In Step With Your Class

Noël Janis-Norton

Barrington Stoke

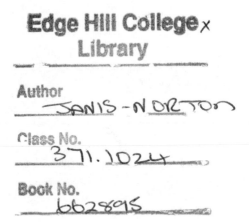
First published in Great Britain by Barrington Stoke Ltd, Sandeman
House, 55 High Street, Edinburgh, EH1 1SR

www.barringtonstoke.co.uk

ISBN 1-84299-217-1

Edited by Julia Rowlandson
Cover design by Helen Ferguson
Typeset by GreenGate Publishing Services, Tonbridge TN9 2RN
Printed in Great Britain by The Cromwell Press

Contents

Acknowledgements

My heartfelt thanks to all the people who have helped make my dream a reality, my friends, colleagues and supporters at The New Learning Centre:

To Robin Shaw, for being the spiritual midwife who made the birth of this book as easy as possible.

To Gillian Edwards, who has been with me through thick and thin, who has enriched this work with her irresistible enthusiasm and who keeps me laughing.

To Miriam Chachamu, for her astute judgment and her commitment to challenging all assumptions.

And to Michael Rose and Gill Dyer, for all their behind the scenes support.

My family:

To my sister Jill Janis, who played a vital role in the development of these ideas, and who teaches these principles at The Family Learning Centre in Tucson, Arizona.

To my children, Jessica, Jordan and Chloé, whose belief in me keeps me going when I forget to believe in myself.

I dedicate this book to the thousands of children, teachers and parents from whom I have learned so much.

Chapter 1
Doing something different to get different results

1. Why I wrote this book

As a trainee teacher observing the more experienced teachers, I was fascinated to discover what they did that worked or did not work to achieve calm, focused learning. I became determined to learn from those teachers' successes and mistakes so that I would not have to experience the frustration and despair that was and still is so prevalent. My strategy was to model myself on the excellent teachers I saw, those whose classrooms were the calmest and the most friendly, with the most time spent teaching and learning and the least time spent on reminding, cajoling, warning, threatening and punishing.

I found that I had to rely on watching and listening very carefully to learn what to do because the excellent teachers did not really know how to put into words what they were doing. Good practices came so naturally to them that they had never needed to try and analyse what they did. So I did the analysing myself as I observed. I put into practice what I learned, and I refined my "Calmer, Easier, Happier Teaching and Learning" methods as I progressed, over time, from classroom teacher to special needs advisor and co-ordinator, head teacher, lecturer, consultant, teacher–trainer and eventually parenting trainer.

One of my purposes in writing this book is to reduce the widespread suffering that I hear about and see when I consult in schools. It is not only teachers who suffer emotionally when we cannot do our job of teaching properly and therefore do not feel successful. Pupils also suffer when they cannot do their "job" properly and therefore do not feel successful as learners. But our pupils do not suffer in silence. They act out their feelings of frustration and failure.

Inclusion is supposed to be part of a solution, but many see it as part of a problem. Sadly, it is the ongoing experience of many teachers that as more and more pupils with special educational needs are being expected to cope in mainstream classes, more pupils are suffering and more teachers are suffering. It does not have to be like this!

I have written this book for all teachers (and prospective teachers, Learning Support Assistants, SENCOs and Learning Mentors, etc) who are on the lookout for new ideas, or a fresh perspective, on how to resolve the growing problems of teaching and how to make the most of every teaching opportunity, both for yourselves and for your pupils.

Teaching pupils to be motivated and co-operative is not accomplished overnight, but in several gradual stages. This book has been organised to delineate the steps that result in pupils becoming motivated and co-operative.

In Chapter 2, I will explore some significant barriers to success, to understand what makes it so difficult for us to achieve our goals for our pupils.

Chapters 3, 4, 5 and 6 are about what we can do every day to prevent problems or reduce their impact: daily practices, ongoing routines and policies and actions that lay the foundations for co-operation and motivation.

In addition, a companion volume, "Learning to Listen, Listening to Learn", shows how the language that teachers use can significantly enhance or undermine the learning, attention and behaviour of our most worrying pupils.

You may feel uncomfortable about my highly directive approach. There are many times in this book when I say, "Do this or that" or "Do not do this or that". If you have pupils whom you are not reaching by what you are already doing, I ask you to keep an open mind and read every chapter before you pass judgement.

2. What teachers are trying to achieve: our goals for our pupils

All teachers have as their goal providing the optimal learning environment for all pupils. In any mainstream classroom a number of pupils will have special needs, whether diagnosed or not, that make it very difficult for them to concentrate, understand, remember and use new skills and information and then successfully transfer the knowledge they have learned to new situations. These pupils' needs must be met in order for them to be able to fulfil their potential.

In addition to goals for academic learning, most of us also have goals for our pupils in the areas of social interaction, communication and values. Regardless of the pupil's personality, the age of the pupil, the ethnic background or his learning style, we want to help each pupil to become a contributing member of the classroom and of society, with positive values, useful skills and habits, and solid self-esteem. We also want our pupils to develop the confidence to strive for and achieve their goals for themselves. We want our pupils to use and to enjoy developing their unique talents, gifts and interests.

In the classroom, pupils have the opportunity to learn many important skills, attitudes and habits:

- how to work and co-operate with others as a team
- tolerance and understanding
- how to concentrate without being distracted
- acceptance of authority
- how to follow group instructions
- how to ask useful questions
- how to work independently
- self-reliance and common sense
- how to set a good example to peers
- how to give help to, and accept help from, peers.

This is a tall order! In order for these complex skills to be learnt, we need to have a very clear idea of how we will achieve this huge task. Every aspect of the school day needs to be examined, then carefully structured, and re-structured. Very, very little can be left to chance, mood, whim, custom, tradition or habit.

3. What teachers need from pupils in order to achieve these goals

In the narrowest sense, our job description as teachers is about imparting information and skills. When we have successfully taught a pupil something (usually a fact or a skill), he has then learned it, by which we generally mean that he is able to communicate what he knows coherently, by speaking or writing or doing something with his knowledge.

Many of us went into teaching assuming that teaching and learning were quite straightforward activities: we would teach and the pupils would learn. After only a short period of scrabbling at the chalk-face, we came to realise that there were certain fundamental pre-requisites for teaching and learning. Before we can teach we need to have a classroom at least calm and quiet enough to be able to hear ourselves think. Our pupils need to "learn how to learn" so that they do not continually distract themselves and others.

The "Calmer, Easier, Happier Teaching and Learning" method has at its core the training of pupils in the habits that result in school success. These are habits of action, and they lead to habits of thought and even habits of feeling.

The teachers who attend my workshops frequently tell me how frustrating it is to teach pupils who are not ready, willing and able to learn. They have a long "wish list":

- respect for authority
- co-operation
- self-esteem
- confidence
- maturity
- common sense
- social skills
- motivation
- enjoyment of learning
- tolerance
- doing one's best
- willingness
- engagement
- self-reliance.

These words are vague, and can mean different things to different people. To make these wishes come true we need to know exactly what we mean. I often ask teachers, "What would it *look like* on the outside, what could an observer *see*, if a particular pupil were feeling respectful or engaged or self-confident?". Time and again I hear the same responses from teachers. The fine, vague phrases above usually boil down to the following five habits:

- Act politely, considerately and positively which includes:
    - eye contact
    - listening
    - helping others, not laughing at others' mistakes.
- Follow instructions immediately (without arguing or asking for exceptions).
- Remember and follow rules and routines with very few prompts.
- Stay on-task.
- Pay attention to all the details of the task, which is a more precise way of saying "doing one's best".

Most teachers tell us they would be very happy if their pupils developed these five habits because these are the habits which enable pupils to enjoy learning, to apply themselves and to achieve their potential, whatever their potential might be. And, of course, the presence of these five habits makes teaching a pleasure!

4. The range of pupils in a typical classroom

A few pupils in every classroom are a joy to teach. They may not even be particularly able academically, but they are enthusiastic and they manage to control their impulses most of the time. The majority of pupils are neither highly motivated nor highly disruptive, neither very easy nor very difficult.

The techniques outlined in this book will certainly help all these pupils to do and be their best. But you and I know that we do not really need any new techniques to deal with these pupils because these pupils are relatively *easy*. They are fun to teach. But often we are too busy fire-fighting the behavioural issues to give these pupils what they need and deserve. You may feel guilty knowing that some of these pupils could really forge ahead if they got more of your attention. Don't you wish you could spend more time with these pupils?

At the other end of the spectrum, you probably have in your class a handful (or possibly several handfuls!) of pupils who are the exact opposite of easy. Everything is a "big deal" to them; just getting them to follow instructions and rules is a daily struggle. Trying to manage their behaviour takes up an inordinate amount of your time. One beleaguered teacher who attended a "Calmer, Easier, Happier Teaching and Learning" workshop described these pupils as "like a black hole that sucks in all my time and attention and strategies, with very, very little to show for it".

One typical characteristic of the middle majority in your classroom is that they are easily influenced. Many teachers have noticed that these pupils start the beginning of the school year relatively focused and well-behaved, but as the weeks and months go by they gradually become noisier, more careless, less attentive and less respectful. Here is one of the reasons I have identified for this upsetting turn of events. The negative attitudes and behaviour of the few "difficult" pupils set an exciting, appealing example to the majority who would not, ordinarily, have thought of behaving badly. This is a particularly potent influence when pupils can see that not much happens by way of consequences, other than being told off or shouted at, when the difficult pupils are unco-operative or disrespectful. Over time, negative behaviour becomes more and more the norm in the eyes of all the pupils, not just the especially challenging pupils. The classroom atmosphere can deteriorate alarmingly.

Even having only a few pupils with behavioural problems in each class is enough to make a teacher's job very stressful because the constant balancing act produces uncomfortable feelings in the teacher:

- tension
- frustration
- anxiety and worry
- resentment and anger
- feelings of failure.

5. Why widespread misbehaviour exists

Why is there such a widespread lack of co-operation and motivation?
Many different reasons have been suggested:

- dysfunctional families
- parents not spending enough time with their children
- violent role-models in the media
- poor nutrition
- society's lack of respect for teachers
- society's emphasis on materialism
- overcrowded classrooms
- teachers demoralised by mountains of paperwork
- teacher–training that does not adequately prepare teachers for the reality of the classroom
- the negative influence of television on standards of literacy
- etc, etc – add your favourite reasons!

In addition to all those reasons, I would like to add:

- Many pupils have not been trained at home to accept the authority of their parents; therefore, they do not automatically assume that they should co-operate with adults who are in charge of them.
- They are confused, overwhelmed, frustrated or resentful because their school work is too difficult for them, and they have felt like failures for a long time.
- They have received too much criticism and lecturing and not enough praise and experience of success.
- They are preoccupied with problems that would interfere with even a mature adult's ability and willingness to pay attention (bullying and teasing, parents arguing, worries about their sexuality, etc).

But here is what I would like to put at the top of the list: many problems with co-operation and motivation are caused by schools not knowing how to meet the needs of pupils who have subtle specific learning difficulties. Pupils who experience difficulties with learning gradually become disaffected, switched off, bored, and resentful. As time goes by, they attract more and more criticism, and many carve out a niche for themselves. It is as if they say to themselves, "I can never be good, so I will become the best at being bad". Teachers may say of these pupils, "he's looking for trouble" or "he's itching for a fight". And they are right! These pupils are fighting back, and what is at stake is their self-esteem.

6. Underpinning concepts of "Calmer, Easier, Happier Teaching and Learning"

a. starting point versus excuses

b. influence versus control

c. motivation versus will-power

d. way of life versus menu

e. investment versus sacrifice.

6a. Starting point versus excuses

All pupils can learn and improve. But both in terms of learning and of behaviour, we will never know the upper limits of what a child can be and do. So we need always to keep our focus on helping him to master the next small step.

The time frame within which a pupil can achieve any goal will be determined by multiple factors, some of which are within the teacher's control and some of which are not. It never benefits the pupil to rush him through work that is taking him longer to absorb and remember than he, his parents, the school, or the National Curriculum think it should take him. So stop yourself if you are getting caught up in unrealistic expectations for your pupil. Accept your pupil for what he is and is not and for where he is and is not.

6b. Influence versus control

As much as we might like to at times, we cannot control our pupils' behaviour. We cannot force them to do the right thing. You have probably tried and found that it does not work, at least not for very long. Certainly, traditional punishments are not effective; the same pupils keep getting punished. After a while the number of detentions racked up becomes a badge of honour. Even shouting, a last resort of which teachers are not proud, does not work to control persistent misbehaviour.

What does work is influencing pupils to change their habits. Influence is all about gradual changes over time, although not necessarily a long time. Teachers consistently report that putting all these new ideas into practice simultaneously usually results in visible, demonstrable behavioural and academic improvements within two to four weeks. That's hard to believe at first. How can hard-core, persistent troublemakers be transformed into law-abiding citizens in a month or less? Unfortunately, that is not what I am promising. You will see very positive changes within two to four weeks, but you will not be out of the woods yet. The longer you carry on using the new skills, the more solid and far-reaching the changes in your pupils will be.

But when we forget to use the new skills, the positive results will quickly fade, and problems with co-operation and motivation will resurface.

6c. Motivation versus will-power

We have all experienced the strange phenomenon of sometimes being able to "make" ourselves do something difficult or scary or tedious, while at other times we cannot seem to "make" ourselves do it. Will-power is very unreliable (as all dieters know only too well). Our pupils are, by definition, immature. And the difficult pupils are even more than usually immature, impulsive and distractible. So they are even less able to summon up the will-power to make the behavioural changes we ask of them, even when they sincerely want to comply and stay out of trouble. So let's stop expecting them to be able to do it just because we tell them to. Instead of exhorting our pupils to do the right things and to stop doing the wrong things and then getting frustrated when they don't, we can harness the power of motivation.

Motivation is about making it easy for pupils to please us, which automatically results in their wanting to please us more and more. You may feel that children and teenagers should be motivated from within, that they should want to do the right thing simply because it is right. That kind of mature motivation is out of the reach of most children and even many teenagers. Developmentally, the stages of motivation are:
1. imitation
2. desire to please the adults who care about them
3. being true to what you believe is right because it feels better.

Most pupils are still at stages one and two.

6d. Way of life versus menu

You could think of the ideas presented in this book as a menu from which you can select the ones that appeal to you most. This approach, however, will not achieve the results we all want: calmer, easier, happier teaching and learning.

All these ideas hang together as a unified methodology. Therefore, I ask you to view these ideas more as a way of life than as a menu.

6e. Investment versus sacrifice

When we invest, we expect to get something back. In this book, I am not asking you to do things differently because the new ways are "right", but because you will get something back when you use them. Whenever you feel that these new methods are too hard to learn or too hard to keep up, remember: this is an investment that will pay off, over time, in calmer, easier, happier teaching and learning, better behaviour and fewer grey hairs.

7. Forging new habits

The not-so-good news is that we are going to have to change our habits and learn to do things differently if we want to get different results. This may seem a daunting prospect, but many of the techniques are familiar to you already. What may be unfamiliar is the degree of consistency we advocate.

The techniques I discuss in this book are all common sense. However, you have probably heard the saying: "The trouble with common sense is that it's not very common.". The techniques I talk about are simple to describe and grasp, but *not easy* to put into practice, especially at first.

8. A frequently asked question

Here is a question I have been asked many, many times:

"I'm far too busy and stretched already, and overwhelmed with all these government initiatives. How can I possibly find the time to try a bunch of new techniques?"

My reply:
I would like to reply to this question with a question of my own to you: wouldn't you have *more time* for teaching plus a much less stressful work day, if the three or four most annoying pupils in your class (or classes) were not so disruptive? Imagine if you did not have to face, day after day, the repeated:

- interruptions and unnecessary questions
- arguing, complaining, refusing to follow instructions
- insulting and teasing of classmates
- "forgetting" to follow rules and routines
- asking for exceptions; being willing to comply only on their terms
- doing the bare minimum, and even that only when the teacher is right next to them
- "learned helplessness".

In our "Calmer, Easier, Happier Teaching and Learning" workshops, when we pose this question to teachers, the usual response is something like this:

> "Of course, it would be wonderful! But it's not possible. If such a miracle were to occur:
> - I'd feel like I could finally do the job I was hired to do, instead of putting so much effort into crowd control.
> - I wouldn't feel so tense by the end of the day.
> - I could really enjoy my weekends, instead of using them to recuperate.
> - I wouldn't feel like such a failure."

As teachers, we all like to think that we are positive, firm and consistent, or that we would be, if only our circumstances were better (smaller classes, new text books, politer pupils, fewer administrative duties, higher salaries, etc). Most teachers are naturally positive, firm and consistent with the co-operative pupils because it is easy to be. However, it is much harder to be positive, firm and consistent with the pupils who don't respect our authority, don't pay attention, don't listen, don't follow our instructions and who don't do the work we set for them. This book aims to make reaching and teaching these pupils easier.

9. My use of gender pronouns

The pronoun "he" is used exclusively in this book when I am referring to a pupil, solely because more than three-quarters of all pupils with learning and behaviour problems are boys. The pronoun "you" refers in all cases to the teachers, learning support assistants and parents who are reading this book.

Chapter 2
Obstacles to learning

1. How we learn

Because there are so many different diagnoses under the general category of "special educational needs" (and more being coined every year), it seems at first glance as if there are many different problems that the classroom teacher must learn to handle. But in fact there is a huge amount of overlap amongst the disorders. In terms of what they need from us, these pupils are more like each other than they are like the pupils who do not have special educational needs.

Most of the diagnoses boil down to attempts to describe or define how a child learns well and how he does not learn well. People take in information through the five sensory modalities or processing channels:

- visual
- auditory
- kinesthetic (movement as well as touch)
- taste
- smell.

Most people take in information better through one or two of these channels and less well, or even not well at all, through one or two of the other channels.

All of us feel most comfortable and are most successful when we use our strongest processing channel, so, of course, we use it the most and come to rely on it. That channel becomes even stronger and more skilled. And because we feel less comfortable and are less successful when we use our weaker processing channels, we avoid using them, whenever possible. The weaker processing channels get less of a workout so they may become even weaker. Over time, this combination of the channels we tend to use and the ones we tend not to use becomes our own unique "learning style".

Many pupils with specific learning difficulties and neuro-behavioural disorders have some variation of the following learning style:
- relatively strong kinesthetic processing
- poor auditory processing
- visual processing may be strong, average or weak, but is generally stronger than the auditory.

Why do processing weaknesses lead to academic difficulties, behaviour problems and emotional vulnerability?
- The pupil is processing slowly and laboriously, so he is likely to miss new information while he is struggling to absorb and understand the previous information or instruction.
- This pupil has a shortened attention span because continued processing with a weak channel feels uncomfortable; the child's mind naturally drifts to a more enjoyable or rewarding thought or activity.
- This pupil tires quickly, loses motivation, concentration, optimism and energy. Even after rest or a break, he does not bounce back quickly.
- Embarrassment or shame about not feeling successful further interferes with the pupil's capacity to concentrate, understand and remember.
- Over time, this pupil becomes more and more easily upset as he comes to view himself as a failure.
- The many inevitable frustrations of his school day often leave this pupil feeling depressed, irritable, angry, and possibly defensive or even defiant – even before anything has gone wrong that day.

For all these reasons, pupils with processing weaknesses are often called "atypical learners" or "non-traditional learners", to distinguish them from their classmates who are able to learn more easily in a typical classroom. Next, let's look in detail at how auditory processing weaknesses can effect learning and attention.

2. Auditory processing weaknesses

Many problems with learning, attention and behaviour are caused by or exacerbated by auditory processing deficits. This is because school activities typically require pupils to pay close attention to what the teacher is saying, to understand multi-layered explanations and to follow complex instructions. When a pupil has weak auditory processing, many aspects of school become difficult, tedious and unrewarding.

Pupils with receptive or expressive language difficulties are confused about the many functions of language. They 'describe' when they are asked to 'define'. They say things like, "Movement means when you move around." and find it very hard to understand why a definition cannot logically include the word they are trying to define. They 'narrate' when they are asked to 'explain'. When they are describing, they dwell on irrelevant details and miss out the significant features. When they are explaining, they leave out important information because they do not have a clear understanding of what is called "shared background knowledge".

Do not assume that a pupil whose hearing has been tested and pronounced "normal" can hear properly. Many pupils with learning deficits and/or social difficulties turn out to have problems hearing certain speech frequencies or discriminating between certain sounds.

The pupil with auditory processing weakness is often a better visual learner, which means that he pays attention to and understands and remembers what he sees better than what he hears. He may be good at visualising (making vivid and detailed mental pictures). But he may well have to be taught how to turn what he hears into mental pictures.

The following checklist of true or false statements can be used to help the pupil, his teachers and his family to understand what he finds difficult and why.

Characteristics of auditory processing weaknesses

Checklist for pupil

Mostly Mostly
TRUE FALSE

❑ ❑ It seems I have to ask people to repeat what they've said a lot.

❑ ❑ I find myself tuning out in classes when the teacher talks a lot, even when I try to pay attention.

❑ ❑ Often I know what I want to say, but I can't find the right words.

❑ ❑ People say I talk with my hands.

❑ ❑ My parents say I started talking late.

❑ ❑ I have trouble understanding if someone turns their back to me while talking, or covers their mouth.

❑ ❑ It's easier for me to look and see what everyone else is doing than to figure it out from the teacher's instructions.

❑ ❑ When I watch television or listen to music, people ask me to turn down the volume.

❑ ❑ I'm told I say "huh?" or "what?" a lot.

❑ ❑ I am not good at giving verbal explanations or directions.

❑ ❑ Words that sound alike, such as bill and bell, give me trouble.

❑ ❑ I have trouble remembering things unless I write them down.

❑ ❑ Sometimes I mistakenly say things like "he got expended from school", and everyone but me thinks it's funny.

❑ ❑ My notes have lots of pictures, arrows and underlinings.

❑ ❑ I like art better than music.

❑ ❑ I have to start from the beginning of the alphabet to remember whether "m" comes before or after "r".

continued

Mostly Mostly
TRUE FALSE

❏ ❏ I'm not good at memorising.

❏ ❏ I make weird mistakes in spelling, like "hate" for "hat".

❏ ❏ I'm no good at sounding words out, but I can figure them out from the story.

❏ ❏ Before I follow directions, it helps me to see someone else do it first.

❏ ❏ I get lost or am late if someone <u>tells</u> me how to get to a new place and I didn't write down the directions.

❏ ❏ When trying to remember someone's telephone number, or something new like that, it helps me to get a picture of it in my head.

❏ ❏ If I am taking a test, I can "see" the textbook page and where the answer is.

❏ ❏ It helps me to <u>look</u> at the person when I am listening. It keeps me focused.

❏ ❏ It's hard for me to understand what a person is saying when there are other people talking or music is playing.

❏ ❏ It's hard for me to understand a joke when someone tells me.

❏ ❏ It is better for me to get work done in a quiet place.

❏ ❏ When I can't think of the word I want to say, I'll use my hands or call something a "what-cha-ma-call-it" or a "thingy".

❏ ❏ My teacher talks too fast, so I get confused.

❏ ❏ I wish the teacher would keep the class quiet; otherwise I can't concentrate properly.

3. Observable characteristics of "atypical" learners

Teachers find that regardless of their diagnoses, many pupils who are experiencing problems with learning, attention or behaviour (whether in the classroom, in the playground or in the corridors) have problems in the following areas:

LEARNING

Concentration

These pupils are highly distractible. This is often because they cannot understand spoken language as quickly as the teacher is talking. It can also be that their need for kinesthetic or visual stimulation continually tempts them away from the task at hand.

Organisation

- loses things
- does not bring in homework or equipment on the right day
- forgetful, even about things that matter to him
- does not seem to see the difference between a tidy desk or an untidy one.

Sequencing (ordering)

Long after the usual age, this pupil is still confused about:
- seasons, months, days of the week
- yesterday and tomorrow
- the alphabet
- poor sense of time, e.g., "Have we had lunch yet, Miss?".

Short-term memory and "working memory"

It is especially difficult for this pupil to hold several pieces of new information in his head at the same time. This is the pupil who will repeat the same mistake right after he has been corrected. He may even willingly rub out a wrong answer but then write the wrong answer in again.

He may have an excellent long-term memory for what interests him, but unfortunately not very much school learning gets stored in his long-term memory. Because information keeps falling out of the short-term memory, it does not stick around long enough to get transferred into the long-term memory.

Spoken language

Problems occur in:
- immature or disordered language, or both
- this oddness can result in isolation, rejection, teasing or bullying.

Reading

Even in secondary school, this pupil still has problems with:
- accurate decoding
- reading with expression and fluency
- comprehension.

Writing

Often, the work set is:
- difficult for this pupil to understand in the way it is presented, although the material could be understood if presented through the pupil's stronger processing channel
- too long for this pupil's attention span
- hurried, which adds to this pupil's frustration, anxiety and resentment.

The result of these conditions is often work that is poorly done, sketchy, with lots of blanks; we know that the pupil is not learning anything useful. The worst-case scenario is that the work is not done at all. Occasionally, almost by a fluke, the work is done to an acceptable standard.

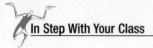

BEHAVIOUR AND SOCIAL SKILLS

Lots of time off-task

Which is often due to:
- impulsivity and distractibility
- immaturity
- heightened sensitivity to the environment
- attention-seeking
- low self-esteem.

Aggression and anxiety

These seem to be flip sides of the same coin. Just think of a wild animal being chased; when it is finally cornered and cannot escape, it instinctively turns to face its pursuer and lashes out ferociously. Some pupils with problems are trying to "escape"; others are "lashing out".

Egocentricity

- very self-absorbed
- only sees his point of view

Narrow interests and fixations

- often knows a great deal about one or two topics
- does not really know how to carry on a conversation; tends to dominate with talk of his "specialist subject"

Inflexibility

- is easily upset when things do not go his way
- is very unsettled by unexpected changes

Immature social skills

- is not aware of his effect on others
- does not understand the need for sharing or turn-taking

Unrealistic

- wildly over-estimates or under-estimates
- misjudges
    - how people will react to what he does
    - who his friends are
    - how long tasks will take
- denies his faults, but also denies his good qualities

Class clown

Many a class clown has explained to me that when other pupils laugh at what he says or does that means they are his friends. Being the class clown is often an attempt to buy friendship by a pupil who does not have the social skills needed to maintain friendships. Sometimes being the class clown is a way to get back at teachers, who may come to be seen as the enemy.

Learned helplessness

Believing that he is not capable, so not even trying.

Fear of failure and success

It is easy to see that fear of failure is born from the experience of failure. Interestingly, fear of success also arises out of the experience of failure. Sometimes teachers are guilty of holding a pupil's successes against him:

"I know you can finish you work on time because you did it last week so that you would be allowed to go on the school trip."

"Finally! See, that wasn't so bad!"

"Why can't you be like this all the time?"

It may seem more comfortable to this beleaguered pupil to stay in the wrong rather than to try and "be good" and somehow still get criticised. Sometimes it becomes a matter of saving face. The pupil would rather be told off for not trying than be told off for trying and getting it wrong.

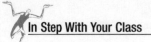

Low self-esteem

This is a result of all the criticism that the problem behaviour understandably attracts.

Heightened emotional reactions

- Confusion, when the pupil is told off for doing what he thought he was told to do.
- Embarrassment when his mistakes are commented on publicly.
- Frustration when he is not making himself understood.
- Feelings of shame when he can see that others, no brighter than he is, understand and remember and succeed, but he does not seem to be able to.
- Angry, anxious or depressed when he is criticised or laughed at.

How do pupils express these very uncomfortable feelings?

- motivation, enthusiasm and energy for learning gradually evaporates
- non-co-operation seeps in:
  - avoidance
  - attention-seeking
  - defiance

A. Avoidance tactics – passive resistance

- Deliberate idleness.
- Complies only when the teacher is watching.
- "Goes through the motions" but doesn't do his best.
- Will not proof-read or else he says he has, after only a cursory glance.
- Doesn't seem to "remember" repeatedly stated expectations (e.g. neatness counts, show all the steps in a maths problem, indent beginning of paragraphs, use complete sentences).
- Does not participate much in class.

Pupils continue to be non-compliant when they have been allowed to "get away with it". They will cleverly take advantage of any weakness in

Chapter 3

Creating a positive, firm and consistent culture in your classroom

1. Why it is so important to be positive, firm and consistent

I am convinced (based on my own experiences, my observations of teachers and the reports I have had back from teachers who have used the "Calmer, Easier, Happier Teaching and Learning" techniques), that one of the keys to successful inclusion is the establishment of a positive, firm and consistent "culture" in every classroom. By this I mean that we, the teachers, need to have as our priority being positive, firm and consistent.

By positive I mean:
- friendly
- calm
- smiling
- not shouting or criticising
- preparing for success rather than letting things go wrong and then over-reacting.

Firm in this context means:
- following through on your decisions
- having the patience that comes from determination
- being steady, constant, unyielding.

Consistent means continuing to be positive and firm, even when it is extremely tempting to become negative or wishy-washy. Consistency is needed at every stage:
- preparing for success = prevention of problems
- nipping potential problems in the bud = early intervention
- containment or damage limitation = managing conflict.

the authority structure, any loopholes in the school's policies or cracks in what should be a united front amongst the teachers and the administration. These pupils will try to wriggle out of following instructions, and if they manage to be "successful" at it even a percentage of the time, they will feel that it is worth trying to wriggle every single time, just in case this is one of the times that wriggling works. This pattern is often habitual and usually quite unconscious, so that the pupil is often not even aware that a huge part of his energy and intelligence is being devoted to trying to get away with things, rather than to co-operating and learning.

B. Attention-seeking – slightly more active resistance
- Complaining
- Blurting out
- Showing off
- Bothering other pupils
- Interrupting
- "Telling on" others pupils
- Asking unnecessary questions

This is the pupil who, in earlier days, was called: smart Alec, loud mouth, lippy, wise guy. Now we might say he has an "attitude" or "pushes our buttons". Whatever words we use to describe this pupil, we sense he is constantly testing us.

All pupils seek and deserve positive attention. If they are not getting enough positive attention, they soon learn how to get negative attention. The easiest way for pupils to get negative attention is *not* to do what they are told. All teachers have observed that many children and teenagers would rather receive negative attention than no attention at all. What might seem hard to accept is that in most classrooms it is far easier for pupils to get negative attention from the teacher than it is to get positive attention. We have all been guilty of it: when pupils are doing what they should be doing, a busy teacher may hardly even "register" the compliance, and often feels in too much of a hurry, too stressed or preoccupied, to stop and praise. But when pupils do not co-operate that throws a spanner in the works and interrupts the smooth flow of classroom routines, so we definitely notice and say something about it. In most classrooms there are a few pupils who seem locked into an irritating and depressing downward spiral: misbehaviour leads to criticism and less praise, which leads to more misbehaviour, and then to more criticism, *ad infinitum*. When children and teenagers are caught in this vicious circle, only the adults can change the direction.

C. Outright defiance and refusal – very active resistance

- Aggressive body language
- Saying "I won't, you can't make me"
- Swearing
- Not doing homework
- Truanting
- Storming out of the classroom
- Violence or threats of violence

Luckily, in each school, there are not many children and teenagers who will go so far as to actually defy the *combined strength, certainty and mutual support* of their teachers' united front. Most behaviour that seems like defiance and refusal actually falls into categories A (Avoidance tactics) or B (Attention-seeking) above. As you follow the suggestions in this book, you will notice that the defiance will steadily lessen.

Continual defiance and refusal are often signs that the pupil sees himself as so unsuccessful that he no longer feels he has anything to lose. The teacher–pupil relationship and often the parent–child relationship may be in serious trouble. For example, the pupil may no longer feel capable of pleasing parents or teachers. Or the pupil's behaviour may be a "cry for help", an unconscious attempt to force the adults in his life to do something about very painful problems or tensions. The anxiety or the lack of confidence or the despair that a troubled or troublesome pupil feels can often be hidden under vast amounts of angry or disrespectful behaviour: rude, argumentative, inconsiderate, sullen, provocative, loud, etc. You've probably seen, and heard, it all!

If co-operation, motivation and respect are missing, several things happen in the classroom:

- Pupils will not try to learn; therefore they will not learn well. This is true because academic learning requires real effort and concentration.
- Pupils will be passively or actively resistant to being taught.

Within a remarkably short space of time, pupils respond to this positive, firm and consistent culture by becoming calmer, more willing, more sensible and more tolerant.

Here are some important points to keep in mind about laying the foundations of a positive, firm and consistent classroom environment:

- There are many everyday practices to choose from, and you already have your own favourites. You will be familiar with many of the ones I discuss in this book, but you may not be using them consistently, especially with your most difficult pupils.
- Some techniques are easier to put into practice than others. Start with three or four of the *hardest* ones! Once you have mastered those, everything else is much easier.
- No single technique by itself is a magic wand that will cure all ills. These techniques form a unified whole, a philosophy rather than a menu. You will not see much improvement if you use only the techniques that appeal to you. Challenge yourself to use the techniques that you do *not* think will work with your pupils.
- Doing these techniques perfectly is not necessary; our aim is continual improvement.
- Many of these techniques require us to change old habits and old ways of thinking. Change is never easy, even when what we are doing now is not working to get us what we want.

Many teachers blame themselves for not being positive enough or firm enough or consistent enough with the most difficult pupils. We think there must be something wrong with us. But I think the real reasons that teachers are not positive, firm or consistent enough, especially with the difficult pupils, are that:

- Teacher-training colleges still tend to assume that pupils come to school ready, willing and able to learn. Therefore, very little emphasis is placed on how to teach the necessary behavioural habits without which learning cannot take place. The result is that teachers are not taught how to deal effectively with difficult or potentially difficult situations.

- Often the school administration does not give teachers the support they need to be able to deal with difficult situations.
- We all live in a world that is long on criticism, blame and negativity but very short on praise, compassion, listening and smiles. In fact, there is a very plausible theory that negativity (pessimism, cynicism, "half-empty" thinking and fault-finding) is an innate, evolutionarily programmed survival mechanism. According to this theory, the cave dwellers who expected problems and were on the lookout for them survived to pass on this trait, whilst the sunny, placid bouquet-gatherers became lunch for a sabre-toothed tiger! We could go so far as to say that lack of consistency seems to be a design flaw bred into human beings.
- Because we have the power of choice, we are constantly choosing, and many of our choices contradict each other. The so-called lower animals, on the other hand, have no such problems. Their behaviour is largely determined by instinctive reactions, so they are very consistent.

Even though it is not easy at first, teachers *can* learn how to apply the principles of being positive, firm and consistent to all pupils, even the most resistant, resentful or apathetic ones. This will help us to gain the respect and trust of our pupils, and will lead to more focused learning and enhanced self-esteem (ours as well as theirs).

2. Being in charge

One of the first steps towards creating a positive, firm and consistent classroom is "being in charge", which has been described in different ways by different people:

- being the captain of your own ship
- being someone the pupils look up to
- being respected
- being "the one in authority"
- being taken seriously
- being the person who determines the tempo
- being "a force to be reckoned with"

- being influential
- being the person whose very presence makes the pupil want to improve or want to do the right thing
- being the person who decides what others should or should not do
- being a teacher whose standards are the norm.

To summarise, we could say that being in charge means actively and consciously making the decisions and the rules and then following through, rather than letting things drift or evolve out of habit, poor organisation, procrastination or giving in to our pupils' often very immature ideas of what they should do and how they should behave. What happens when we are in charge?

- We see clearly how things really are right now.
- We know specifically what we want to achieve – in the lesson, in the classroom, in the playground and in the corridors.
- We think carefully about how to make it happen and we decide what we will do.
- We do what we think will work; we carry out our plan consistently and for long enough.

To be in charge of our classroom, we need to be in charge of all the little details that make up the bigger picture. Letting little details slide is never a good idea because the larger picture is made up of many seemingly insignificant details. Ignoring little details that seem unimportant makes it much harder in the long run to exert our influence.

We need to establish that we are in charge from the very beginning of our relationship with the pupils, and also at the very beginning of *every* lesson. Not only do we need to start as we mean to go on; every day we need to *re-start* every single lesson as we mean to go on.

Of course, life is much easier if we establish our authority from day one. But luckily, it is never too late! I have met many teachers who realised, belatedly, that they had gradually allowed themselves to become fuzzy and inconsistent about following though. With determination and persistence, these teachers soon turned the situation around, got back in charge, became the "captain" of their classroom again. And everyone felt better for it.

Respect is an important aspect of being in charge. When pupils respect the authority of a teacher, they become increasingly motivated to do the five things I identified in Chapter 1, even if they do not yet know how to do these five things well. With ongoing, consistent training these actions will become habits:

- acting politely, friendly and positively
- following instructions
- remembering and following rules and routines, with very little prompting
- staying on-task (which includes controlling their impulses)
- paying attention to details.

Therefore, the most important job of teachers and indeed the first job of teachers is to gain respect by being in charge. This will automatically generate enough motivation for learning to start taking place.

Research has shown that respect for authority is based on several different aspects of the teacher–pupil relationship:

> a. awareness
>
> b. care
>
> c. follow-through.

a. Awareness

The teacher knows about that particular pupil:

- his likes and dislikes
- his strengths and weaknesses
- his home circumstances
- the teacher knows what is happening in the lesson, even when the pupil is not in the direct line of vision.

b. Care

The pupil knows from experience that:

- the teacher likes that particular pupil
- the teacher wants the best for that particular pupil
- the teacher has more experience, maturity and wisdom than the pupils have
- the teacher is quick to listen and slow to judge.

c. Follow-through

The pupil knows from experience that you will do what you said you would do.

The pupil knows from experience that the teacher will do something (not just say something) about:
- breaking of rules
- bending of rules.

Some of the rules most often broken include those about:
- calling out instead of raising hand
- name-calling
- not doing homework
- swearing
- chewing gum
- unexcused absence or lateness
- smoking.

In the above list, I have purposefully included examples of minor as well as major rule-breaking to emphasise that a rule is a rule. Even minor rules must be enforced if we want our pupils to take the major rules seriously.

If your school has rules that you feel are not important enough to warrant spending time following through on, we advise you to work to abolish those rules. In the meantime, uphold even those rules you strongly disagree with. Any rule that is not enforced is very harmful to pupil morale because it undermines how the pupils view rules in general. Pupils start guessing which teachers care about which rules, and who will let them "get away with" what. This is the opposite of respect for authority.

Therefore, I strongly suggest that it is in our interest to follow through consistently on all rules, even the ones that do not seem remotely important to us. Plus, it serves as an excellent training in "real life" for our pupils; as they get older they will often be required to comply with rules and expectations that they do not see the point of. They will take this in their stride far more easily if their school experiences have been consistent.

Rule-bending can be frustratingly subtle. The pupil obeys the "letter of
the law" but violates the "spirit of the law". Typical examples of rule-
bending are:

Behaviour:
- grabbing or pushing
- rude tone of voice
- not answering when the teacher asks a question
- not looking at the teacher when the teacher is talking
- fiddling with objects
- slouching
- following instructions the second or third time he is told,
  instead of straightaway
- testing, e.g. "But you never said we couldn't climb on the
  scaffolding.".

Academic performance:
- careless handwriting
- not answering all the questions
- doodling in the margins of homework
- using paper ripped out of a binder
- writing less than required
- printing out pages from the internet and handing it in as part
  of his coursework
- not writing homework down in his planner
- writing one-word answers when instructed to write full
  sentences.

Many pupils are very willing to listen to us and take us seriously. At home
they (mostly!) listen to their parents, so they naturally transfer that same
respect and sense of deference to their teachers. We do not have to work
very hard to get their respect. But with others it is much harder work.
However, even when pupils come to school expecting to do as they please
because they do not respect the authority of their parents, teachers can
gain the pupils' respect. But it will be harder because we will need to be
more careful and more consistent in everything we say and do to ensure
that we are demonstrating awareness, care and follow-through.

Because the pupil must experience the teacher being aware, caring and following through, it follows that the teacher must demonstrate these attitudes through actions, rather than just talking about them. Teachers can only gain the respect of their pupils, can only become the authority and get back in charge, through what teachers do, not through what teachers say or wish or feel or believe.

My experience has shown me that teachers who gain the respect of their pupils through demonstrating awareness, care and follow-through can turn around even very tough, hostile or apathetic children and teenagers.

For pupils to respect the authority of teachers, the awareness, the care and the follow-through must be evident every day. A teacher who lacks awareness, who is not "on top" of what is happening, often ends up with a reputation amongst the pupils for being unfair because it is easy to blame the wrong person unless you cultivate the skill of having "eyes in the back of your head". A teacher who is caring but does not follow through consistently will be deemed weak and will be taken advantage of. A teacher who follows through without actively demonstrating caring will be seen as harsh or heartless and will be resented.

In other words, many pupils nowadays need to be shown and convinced that teachers are worth respecting. This is very different from the traditional attitude to authority prevalent several generations ago, or even several decades ago. Back then, in the "good old days", children and teenagers looked up to adults and looked forward to becoming adults. Nowadays, many teens and even pre-teens already have many of the choices, rights and privileges that were once reserved for adulthood: freedom to dress as they please, plenty of money to spend on themselves, freedom to decide about their social life and entertainment, etc. They no longer yearn to be adults or automatically look up to the adults in their lives.

We need to remember that everything a teacher says or does, and everything a teacher doesn't say or doesn't do, will either improve or undermine discipline. All of the following suggestions are designed to demonstrate to pupils that teachers do follow-through on inappropriate behaviour and that teachers do know their pupils and like them and know what is best for them.

From the very beginning, make sure your tone of voice is authoritative though kind. Maintain a no-nonsense position, even while being friendly or humorous. Remember that it is the teacher who sets the tone of the lesson. The teacher must be in charge at all times.

Part of caring is practising not taking a pupil's reactions (or over-reactions) personally. When a pupil has an uncomfortable feeling (e.g. frustration, anxiety, anger, depression, grief, loneliness), it can make us feel uncomfortable. In the companion volume, "Learning to Listen, Listening to Learn", I discuss the technique of Reflective Listening, which we can use to help our pupils learn to deal positively with their emotions without adding our own upset to them.

Spend some enjoyable individual time with each pupil every day. This builds a strong, positive teacher–pupil relationship, and helps the pupil want to please the teacher. One example of how you can do this: at the beginning of the day, and each time the class enters the room, have the pupils line up in the corridor and come in one by one. That way you can say a positive word or two to each one as they file in, setting a tone of calm, optimism and focus on learning.

3. Distinguishing between pupils' wants and needs

In order to understand what is really happening with our pupils, we need to distinguish between their *wants* and their *needs*.

What a pupil wants and what he needs is very often not the same thing at all. It is our job as teachers to determine what is best for each pupil, in other words, what he *needs* from school.

We can distinguish between our pupils' wants and needs by remembering that apart from the obvious physical needs (food, clothing and shelter), what our pupils really need is:

- to be spoken to respectfully
- to be appreciated
- to be challenged
- to feel successful.

Our pupils need adults who:
- allow them to learn and to make mistakes
- simplify the confusing complexities of life for them by establishing clear expectations
- continue to like them even when they are not being very likeable.

These needs are not transitory; all humans have these needs, even as adults. The quality of a pupil's life will suffer if his needs are not met.

In particular, our most troubled and troublesome pupils need:
- less criticism and more praise
- more individual time with the teacher
- more carefully differentiated work
- training in self-reliance
- more firmness
- consistent consequences.

A pupil's wants can change from moment to moment, and often, paradoxically, the quality of a pupil's life will suffer if his wants *are* met.

Once you have distinguished between a pupil's wants and his needs, the next step is to think carefully (and creatively) about what *you* can do differently in the future to help meet his needs. Do not assume that the problem will just go away! And even if the school did not create the problem, the school can be part of the solution.

Whatever you have been doing so far has not been getting you the results you want. Let's face it: to achieve different results, we will need to do something different.

To help you think constructively about how a particular pupil's needs can be met at school, I suggest that you spend some time with a colleague every day (at least 15 minutes) discussing possible solutions to the problems, but *not* just discussing the problems. You already know what the problems are; do not spend your precious energy rehashing and complaining. Focus on changes *you* can make to achieve a different result. Teachers report that this "solution talk" is useful even when the person you are talking to has no experience of the particular pupil you are discussing.

You may feel that what a particular pupil needs is not so much something from school, but rather something that only the home can provide, e.g. less television, less junk food, parents making the time to supervise homework, etc. However, do not despair! My experience shows that although teachers are in charge of only a portion of the pupil's environment, that portion can become, symbolically, a very *large* influence on a pupil's habits and thoughts. This means that we need to constantly work at putting aside our frustrations about parents who "won't" or "can't" change. Instead, we need to concentrate on what we, as teachers, can do to make school an important focus of values for the pupil. The way to do that is to become more and more *positive, firm* and *consistent*.

4. Preparing for success

Preparing for success means thinking ahead and "acting ahead".

Before the lesson begins

Do not even contemplate teaching a particular skill until the necessary micro-skills have been thoroughly learnt and revised. Otherwise you will be causing confusion and resentment in the pupils, and you may find yourself giving in to the temptation to help too much, explain too many times, etc. Read Chapter 6 for a discussion of micro-skills and how to teach them.

Leave some time in your lesson plan unaccounted for so that you can be spontaneous, pursue a tangential but interesting point, listen to a pupil's rambling tale, etc.

To help you differentiate more and more effectively, build up a personal collection of worksheets and activity sheets which you have found useful. Whenever you find another one to add to your store, make extra copies so that they are available for instant use.

So that you can improvise at a moment's notice, make a list of ideas for group activities that:
- can be completed in 5–20 minutes
- require no preparation or special equipment
- reinforce particular educational concepts or skills
- allow for success regardless of ability level.

Before you let your pupils into the classroom, set up everything you will need *exactly* how it suits you best.

Keep your own area neat, both to set a good example to the pupils and also to avoid hesitation and confusion. Arrange your files, worksheets, records of work, supplies, etc. so that you do not need to rifle through them to find what you need. Investing the time in organising and filing always pays huge dividends in calmness, feeling "on top of things", and being more aware because you are less distracted.

At the beginning of each lesson

Make sure the atmosphere is calm:
- coats, backpacks, bags put away in the proper place
- writing implements, rubbers, etc, out on the desk neatly
- extraneous materials off the table.

Have a routine way of starting each lesson. Make this a silent activity that the pupils can get right down to, without needing any explanations. Writing one-word answers to questions about the current topic, problem-solving exercises, ongoing creative writing and mental arithmetic are all good activities to set a tone of quiet and concentration. This keeps the atmosphere calm and focused. Do not start the lesson with discussion. The opportunity to talk can be used as a reward later on in the lesson.

Insist that pupils take care of toilet visits, drinks of water, etc. before the activity begins. Otherwise they will have to wait for a suitable break, decided on by you.

Recognise that worries and resentments about unresolved issues, whether major or minor, are very strong internal distractions, particularly for the most immature, impulsive, sensitive or intense pupils.

It is pointless to try to teach until the pupils are ready to learn. Trying to is a waste of your valuable time and energy, and it gives the pupils the impression that the teacher's job is to *force* them to work, and that the pupil's 'job' is to resist, delay, distract, wind up, daydream, etc. You can tell when a pupil is ready to learn:

- he is calm
- his desk is orderly and organised
- he is quiet
- he is looking at the teacher waiting for instructions
- he has followed instructions willingly.

See Chapters 4, 5 and 6 for ideas on how to establish these sensible habits. It is just as important for us to teach pupils how to get ready for a lesson, how to focus, how to be organised and receptive, and how to resolve problems, as it is for us to teach academic facts and skills.

Before you begin speaking, take some deep breaths, focus on a calming or energising thought or image, and *smile*.

During the lesson

Smiling a lot helps pupils to feel liked and appreciated. And that motivates them to be more polite, more co-operative and more cheerful.

Allow for every exercise or activity to take longer than you expected. You will often need to spend time calming and focusing the class, generating enthusiasm, listening to problems, revising the micro-skills, guiding your pupils to think sensibly about the instructions, and making sure that all the pupils' questions and concerns have been addressed.

Do not allow pupils to get up and come to you with queries, finished work, etc. This is too distracting for them and for the other pupils. It also unintentionally encourages pupils to drift into the habit of immediately seeking reassurance or help when they are unsure how to proceed. We want to teach them self-reliance. See Chapter 6 for a thorough discussion of how to foster self-reliance.

Vary the format within each lesson or each day, for example, some group discussion or activity, some individual silent work, some work in pairs.

The teacher's positive attitude and enthusiasm contribute greatly to the pupils' motivation. Keep the tone friendly and light. Use humour whenever possible to keep the atmosphere light and to encourage the pupils to be receptive to learning.

Always stop the lesson before the most impulsive pupils become tired or restless. Always end with a success, on an upbeat tone. Each lesson can contain a series of mini-lessons so that several aspects of a topic are taught in any given lesson.

Model the classroom behaviour you are trying to teach: calm, friendly, on-task.

Encourage co-operation; minimise competition. A good motto is: "I co-operate with others, I compete with myself.".

Give an impulsive or resistant pupil a short, easily completed task so that he can experience the satisfaction and boost to his self-esteem that comes from persevering until a goal has been accomplished. A small amount of work done carefully helps to reinforce important lessons, such as the value of patience, accuracy and thoroughness. Only lengthen his tasks as his self-confidence and self-control increase. A larger amount of work that has been "covered", but done carelessly, results in unproductive habits becoming further entrenched.

Allow the pupil to work slowly, if he is really working. Do not expect or ask him to finish by a certain time. Do not hurry him. Either give him a much smaller amount to do so he is likely to finish on time, or plan a time in the future when he can finish it.

Avoid surprise tests; they cause anxiety, confusion, fluster and resentment, with the pupil doing even less well than he might have done with some warning.

To deal with the problem of pupils finishing a task early and then distracting the others, you can assign "waiting work" for pupils, and train them to do this work at *any time* when they are waiting. This work needs to be relevant, easy enough for pupils to do independently and not so attractive that pupils might be tempted to rush their work to get to it.

Examples might be:
- making up sentences using targeted vocabulary
- making up and answering questions on the topic
- reading their current book in absolute silence.

Alternate quiet activities with stimulating ones.

Use a timer to keep pupils focused.

Never give work that is:
- too taxing for his processing, even if he could understand it easily if it were presented differently
- too long for his current attention span
- too rushed (which makes for anxiety, confusion, careless mistakes, passive resistance, procrastination, switching off, learned helplessness or active resistance).

Constantly monitor that pupils are on-task and doing the task correctly.

When very active or impulsive pupils are starting to feel frustrated, before they explode give them a chance to move and a different task that does not require them to use their weaker learning modality.

Limit the number of new concepts presented in any one period. Do not over-stretch or confuse the pupil by trying to have him learn too many things at one time. Introduce new material only after old material has become familiar.

Arrange materials in such a way that the pupil's attention is directed where you want it to be. Teach the pupil to attend to the cues that will facilitate learning, and to learn to disregard those factors in the learning situation that are irrelevant.

Provide success experiences. Pupils who have experienced repeated failure have usually developed low frustration tolerance, negative attitudes towards schoolwork, and possibly some compensatory behaviour problems which make them socially unpopular.

The best way to cope with problems of impulsivity and distractibility is to organise a day-to-day programme presenting the pupil with short-range as well as long-range tasks in which he can succeed. The self-concept of the pupil is largely dependent upon how well he succeeds in the tasks we set him.

Do not distract or interrupt an on-task pupil with irrelevant questions or comments or even corrections. Instead, use Descriptive Praise of something he has done right to guide him to see his mistake. (See Chapter 4)

At the end of the lesson

Wind up the lesson ten minutes before the bell rings to leave plenty of time, not only for setting the homework, but also for clarifying it and for a review of what has been learned or practised.

This winding down is part of the lesson. Some of the most important things we are trying to teach our pupils are how be calm, organised and methodical. Make the last moments you have with your pupils each day calm ones. Aim to become ultra-organised so that you complete the whole winding-down phase with five minutes to spare. You can then play a short educational game or chat with the pupils for the last few minutes.

At least once a day (preferably at the end of the lesson) engage all the pupils in some kind of unifying exercise. This could be wrap-up of the day's work, an educational game, etc. This need not be very time-consuming, but it goes a long way towards building group spirit.

5. Frequently asked questions

There are several typical reactions that teachers have when they first hear my suggestions:

> "A lot of your advice is so obvious that it is almost insulting. Aren't these ideas just common sense? We don't need lists of tips or workshops to learn how to do all this because we are already doing it."

My reply:

Teachers usually are good at putting these principles into practice with the more motivated pupils, but it is easy to get side-tracked, so that we gradually forget about being positive, firm and consistent when faced with difficult pupils, large classes, an overload of administrative details, and so on. We all have weak spots in our methods that need to be strengthened.

"These ideas are wonderful in theory, but too idealistic, too difficult to put into practice because: they slow down the curriculum, they take too much preparation time, classes are too large, and pupils are not co-operative."

My reply:

I know from many years of training teachers that these methods do work, even with pupils who are very troubled and disadvantaged and hostile. Yes, it does *look* like it slows down the curriculum. But when we realise that quite a few pupils in each year are not really learning (understanding, remembering and using the information of skills), then we can readily see that the curriculum *needs* to be slowed for these pupils so that they *can* learn.

"Teachers should not have to earn the respect and trust of pupils. Is it too much to ask that pupils come to school with a healthy respect for authority already instilled in them by their parents and their previous teachers so that we can just get on with the job of teaching?"

My replies:

a) As adults we only respect people who have earned our respect. Children and teenagers are no different.

b) We all wish that pupils would come to school respectful and ready to learn. But since many of them don't, it makes sense for us to tackle the problem, to teach them the essential behavioural micro-skills that can make our job so much easier and more rewarding.

"These ideas about positive, firm and consistent are old-fashioned. Young people are different nowadays, and they won't respond to firmness and accountability. Teenagers just don't care about traditional values any more. How can we get through to them?"

> My reply:
> My experience shows that even tough teenagers respond very well to these methods. Interestingly enough, some of my suggestions may seem too old-fashioned, and some may seem too modern. What I am presenting in this book are common-sense suggestions that have been tried and tested and have been proven to motivate pupils. I ask that you read them with a completely open mind. Start with the frame of mind that says, "These ideas probably do work. I'll use these suggestions in my classroom and see what happens. I have nothing to lose and possibly a great deal to gain."

"I tried some of these methods for a while, but they didn't work. Now what?"

> My reply:
> As teachers, we may try something new but give up too soon when we do not immediately see the results we hoped for. Consistency is the key. We need to leave any new policy in place for two to four weeks before we can accurately judge its effectiveness.

Chapter 4
Descriptive Praise

1. What Descriptive Praise is and is not

Most of the praise we give pupils is "evaluative", for example:
- Well done!
- Good boy! (for the younger child)
- Terrific!
- That's wonderful!
- Super!

One problem with evaluative praise is that the very pupils we are trying to encourage and motivate with our praise are the ones least likely to believe that they are super, wonderful or terrific. They think we do not really mean it but are exaggerating, which is often the truth! Or they think we do mean it and are sadly deluded. But either way, this kind of praise usually does not help pupils to improve. In fact, it can be actually counter-productive, as the pupils with problems grow to distrust what teachers say.

Descriptive Praise, however, is the most powerful motivator and training tool I have ever come across. It helps children and teenagers to want to improve, and it helps them to be able to improve. This technique consists of noticing and mentioning every tiny step in the right direction:
- minor improvements in behaviour or work or social skills
- behaviour or work that is not wonderful or amazing, but just OK (actions that you might think you should be able to take for granted)
- the absence of the negative behaviour.

You will notice that some of the examples of Descriptive Praise are very short, one-sentence responses. These take only a few seconds to utter. Some of the praises are a bit longer because they go into the specifics of what the pupil has done right. And some Descriptive Praises are a whole "paragraph", often involving repetition for maximum impact.

2. We can use Descriptive Praise to improve all aspects of:

A. Behaviour

1. Following instructions

- You did what I asked you to do.
- I told the class to look at the board. I waited and watched, and I saw that every single pupil did it. You all followed my instruction.
- Just now, when I asked the class to put away your homework diaries, I saw that everyone did it. This table (pointing) did it straightaway, and after only a few seconds everyone else's homework diary was also out of sight.
- You did what I told you to do straightaway. I appreciate that.
- I could see that you didn't want to stop what you were doing. You were enjoying yourself, so you wanted to keep going. But it only took you a few seconds to decide to do the right thing. It didn't take you long to follow the instruction.
- You did what you were supposed to do, without any arguing. That shows me that you are co-operating.
- I gave you directions, and you did exactly what I told you to do. You must have been listening really carefully because you didn't leave anything out.
- I gave the class a job to do with three steps to it. When I look around I see that everyone has completed the first step. And this table is on step number two.
- You weren't sure about what my instructions meant, so you put up your hand and asked. And your question was a really sensible question. You didn't just say, "What should I do?" You had your brain switched on, and you were really thinking, so

you only asked about the bit that was confusing you. All the bits that you understood, you had already written down.

Focus your Descriptive Praise on the fact that the pupil co-operated, rather than on whatever the instruction was about.

Some teachers prefer to say "asked" rather than "told" because it sounds less like the teacher is the authority. However, I suggest that teachers *deliberately* use language (including body language) that conveys authority. Experience and research show that pupils are far more likely to co-operate when a teacher habitually conveys authority. In Chapter 3, you will read more ideas on how to make it clear that you, the teacher, are in charge.

2. Following rules and routines

- You remembered our rule, and you followed the rule.
- You remembered what we always do on Monday afternoons, and you did it without having to be reminded. That's self-reliance.
- You told yourself the right thing to do and then you did it. That shows maturity.
- You followed our routine without needing any reminders. You used your common sense.
- You have stayed in your seat for the past 20 minutes. Thank you for following the rule.
- You've stopped tapping. I feel much more peaceful. Now everyone at this table is following the rule about working quietly.
- I see some pupils who are remembering our routine for getting ready to work. You've got your pencil, your ruler and your rubber in front of you. I can see you're ready to work. (Pause) And now I see five more people who are quickly getting ready.
- The rule is to write in silence, and that's exactly what I hear – utter silence. (Said to the whole class or to a group or to an individual pupil.)
- This group is remembering to speak very softly. I appreciate that you're not disturbing any other group.

- The rule about lining up with your hands down is being followed by almost everyone. (Pause) And now even more people are lining up in the correct way.

3. Staying on task

- Several of you looked up when you heard the fire engine go by, but you didn't get out of your seats. You kept on working.
- You're not bothering anyone. That's the way to stay out of trouble.
- That commotion didn't distract you. You kept on writing. Very sensible.
- You've been working for ten whole minutes without any chatting. You're really concentrating.
- I know that writing is definitely not your favourite activity, so I am especially pleased that you stopped complaining.
- Even though you're not sure how to do this sum, you're still working. You haven't given up. I see you're leaving the hardest one until later, and you're working on an easier one first.
- You've told me that you don't feel well, but you're not using it as an excuse to get out of working.
- You've got your pencil in your hand and your exercise book is open. You're about to get down to work.
- You got to school late, but you're making up for lost time. I see you haven't wasted any time. You've already started working.

4. Paying attention to details

- You noticed your own mistake. That's real attention to detail.
- You've got all the right letters, and they're all in the right order. Now you just have to add one silent letter. Aren't silent letters annoying? They turn up when you least expect them.
- On this table I see such an improvement in your presentation. I see titles underlined; I see an invisible margin on the right side of your pages; I see full stops at the end of lots of sentences. Brilliant to see!
- You noticed that I made a mistake. That shows you're really paying attention. And you said it very politely. You didn't sound rude.

5. Acting politely, considerately and positively

- You're waiting patiently.
- Even though you're finished, you're not chatting. You're not disturbing anyone. Thank you.
- You're telling me how you feel about having all this revision over the holidays. And I appreciate that you said it in a polite, respectful voice. It's not always easy to stay calm when you're annoyed.
- You're annoyed, but you're not being rude.
- I am very impressed by how optimistic you are being! You are not sure how this is going to turn out, but you're still smiling.
- You didn't laugh at that mistake.
- You haven't said that you're stupid even once today.
- You probably aren't looking forward to double Maths, but you aren't rolling your eyes or complaining.
- Someone swore at you, and you didn't swear back. That's real self-control.
- You remembered to say thank you, and you didn't need any reminders.
- Thanks for looking me in the eye.
- You all made sure that everyone in your group had a turn.

B. Learning

1. Accuracy

- You've written four sentences, and three of them start with a capital letter. You're remembering the rule.
- You've finished five sums, and four of them are correct.
- That word has all the right letters. You just need to put them in a different order.
- You might not see why I think it's so important to write your answers in full sentences, but I see that you've remembered to do it here and here.

[If the pupil argues and says something like, "I didn't remember; I just did it without thinking", wait a few seconds, and then say something like, "You did it without even having to think about it. That's even better. That means it's becoming a habit."]

- You read that sentence with no mistakes. You didn't rush. You slowed right down, and it paid off. Perfect reading.
- I see you remembered the full stop.

2. Thoroughness

- That answer gives me all the information I need.
- This group has come up with even more examples than you needed to. You didn't stop; you kept on thinking.
- This form that you brought from home has everything filled in – no blanks. Everyone with a permission slip like this will be able to go on the trip.
- Quite a few people have remembered to bring all the materials needed for today's project. Did you find that it was helpful to have that checklist to take home with you?

3. Presentation

- Every letter in this word is sitting exactly on the line.
- I see you've remembered to put only one numeral in each square, just as I asked. That makes it much easier for me to mark.
- Because you have lined up your columns of numbers so neatly, I can easily see if you have added this up correctly.
- It looks like you took a lot of care to dress appropriately for the speeches today: no jeans, no trainers, and you even got your hair cut! You look very professional!

4. Creativity and problem-solving

- You weren't afraid to try a new combination of colours.
- You thought of a new way to show what you learned.

5. Willingness, courage

- You weren't sure how to do that sum, but you had a go. Very brave.
- You didn't say, "I don't know". You took a guess. It takes courage to do that.
- I know you don't like writing, but you're not complaining. That shows me you're growing in maturity.

C. Social skills

1. Turn-taking, patience

- You haven't shouted out in the past 10 minutes.
- You didn't shout out, even though you knew the answer.
- Thanks for not interrupting.
- You're really enjoying this activity, but I see you're remembering to take turns and give someone else a chance.
- On this table no one is arguing about the equipment. I can see that this table is sharing the equipment.
- You want the ball, but you're not grabbing.
- You've been waiting patiently for your turn for five minutes. And when someone tried to jump the queue, you didn't hit or shove. I heard you use your voice. You told him how you felt, and you didn't get into trouble because you didn't use force.

2. Accepting others' views

- I see respect. I see people waiting, not interrupting. This is a very mature discussion.
- You two are having a strong disagreement, but I don't hear any swearing. You're both making a real effort to settle this with sensible words. That's teamwork.
- Even though you disagree with James, you haven't called him "stupid".
- You might be feeling annoyed, but you're keeping it in your head. All I can hear are polite words.

3. Respecting property

- You wanted to use Henry's highlighters, but you controlled yourself. You asked him first if you could borrow them. You respected his property. That's the way to make and keep friends.
- You're not touching anyone else's belongings.
- That pencil was lying there, and you could have taken it, but you didn't because you know it's not yours.
- I noticed that you held onto that wrapper until you found a bin. That's showing respect for the school.
- You remembered to bring your library books back.

4. Helpfulness, teamwork

- I notice several pupils who are assisting others, the way we talked about. How helpful!
- This table has been working together quietly for five minutes. Each person is busy doing something useful. That's teamwork!
- Yesterday, during Maths, I saw many pupils helping other pupils. It was good to see that those who needed help weren't afraid to ask. And it was good to see that those who could help were willing to take the time to do it. I love to see people working together that way!
- This group is developing real solidarity. Completing a big, complicated task together often brings people together like that, haven't you noticed?
- Even though some of you wish you had been assigned different tasks, as a group you pulled together and everything got done. I saw people doing things they didn't really want to do – for the sake of the group.

3. Points to remember about Descriptive Praise

A. General points

- You can use Descriptive Praise when you are tempted to criticise.
  - Don't say: "You're the last one; everyone else has finished".
  - Do say: "You've completed the first three sums".
- Research indicates that people take in, on average, only 30% of what they hear (and remember only 8% after one month!). So saying the same thing in several different ways helps more of your message to sink in.
- At first you will feel awkward, possibly embarrassed. Your words will sound artificial to you. Practice makes progress, but rarely does practice really make perfect.
- At first you may worry that your pupils will laugh or take offence. It will happen occasionally, but far less often than you imagine it will.
- When pupils hear another pupil being Descriptively Praised, it:
  - motivates them to get attention in the same way
  - gives them important information about how to get positive attention.
- When Descriptively Praising, use nouns rather than pronouns. Either repeat the exact same noun or vary it slightly. Using more nouns and far fewer pronouns will make your language sound more formal, more "important" and impressive, less conversational and "ignorable". It will also probably help you slow down your speaking, which has numerous benefits. Slow speech sounds more "important", and pupils with auditory perception problems and/or pupils who are not really listening will take in more of what you say. Also, speaking more slowly will give you the time to choose more interesting and more graphic vocabulary.
- Everyone wants, needs, deserves and thrives on attention. Some pupils are experts in attracting negative attention. Or they may not really know how to control their inappropriate impulses long enough to get much praise. Descriptive Praise for even

fleeting OK behaviour proves to this pupil that he can do it right, as he has just done it. This motivates him to try and control himself a bit more.

- Each Descriptive Praise takes only after a few seconds, which is less time than it takes to tell off, criticise, or deliver a mini-lecture, and it is much more effective at changing habits.

- Use a pupil's name when you Descriptively Praise, but *not* when you correct or criticise. When pupils hear their name connected to a positive comment, it further enhances their self-esteem.

- Descriptive Praise is more motivating than criticism or reminders.

- Whenever you identify a problem that a pupil is having, make a point of finding some small improvements in that area to praise *every day*, even though you may need a magnifying glass to find them! The purpose of this is to demonstrate to the pupil that he is already starting to improve. This gives the pupil something to feel good about and something to live up to, something he knows he can do again because he has already done it before.

  For example, we can say to a forgetful, disorganised pupil: "Thank you for putting your book back on the shelf", or "You haven't called out at all in the last ten minutes; you've been quiet and patient".

- Use praise to make your point; pupils will listen and remember and appreciate it.

- Praise even the tiniest steps in the right direction.

- To get more mileage from one round of Descriptive Praise, start with naming a few pupils who are doing something right. As the ripple effect spreads and more pupils follow their example, mention a table, then the side of the room and eventually the whole class.

- When we are trying to persuade or reason with pupils, our explanations often fall on deaf ears. Instead, get into the habit of giving your reasons and explanations as part of a Descriptive Praise; pupils are far more likely to be "tuned in". For example:

> "Because each person helped clean up, the job got done quickly and thoroughly. We even have time for a game before the bell rings."

> "Just now you brought over enough scissors for everyone at your table. That helped reduce the traffic in the room. Thanks for the extra bit of peace and quiet."

- Praise often.

B. Qualities

Descriptive Praise becomes even more effective if we also mention the quality that the pupil is demonstrating. This helps him to see himself in a different light. Here are some of the qualities that we can notice and mention:

- co-operation
- bravery, courage
- patience
- willingness
- helpfulness, thoughtfulness
- sensible approach
- responsible attitude
- optimism, cheerfulness, sunny side up
- self-control
- attention to detail
- self-reliance
- organisation
- honesty.

After your Descriptive Praise, you might add:

- – That shows me that you are co-operating.
- – Your self-control is improving every day.
- – That was brave of you.
- – You're using your common sense.

When we talk about these qualities, it is better to say "That was" or "That shows", rather than "You are" because the pupil knows he is often *not* that quality, so he could argue about or dismiss a comment that was made about himself as a whole.

4. A frequently asked question

Question:

> "I'm worried that the older pupils will feel patronised if I Descriptively Praise them so much. How can I get them to see that I'm not being condescending or sarcastic?"

> > My reply:
> > Isn't it funny that we seem to worry more about how pupils will react to Descriptive Praise than about how they will react to criticism, lecturing and telling off?
> > Some pupils, especially the ones who have been told off a lot, may feel very uncomfortable with Descriptive Praise at first. Descriptive Praise shakes up their image of themselves and of their world. Teachers have even reported to me that particularly resistant, recalcitrant pupils have complained about the Descriptive Praise at first, saying that they preferred being told off because they knew that was what they really "deserved"! My advice to you is: persevere. Descriptive Praise always helps pupils to see their true worth, but of course it will take some pupils longer than others.

Chapter 5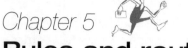
Rules and routines

1. Rules we make for ourselves

When we focus on rules, we immediately think of rules that our pupils need to follow. As important as these are, what are even more important are the rules we make for ourselves. The rules we set for our own behaviour will largely determine whether we feel on top of our job or swamped by it. And even though it is often not easy to make ourselves do what we think we should do, it is certainly much easier than trying to get someone else to follow rules we make for them. So let us keep our attention fixed firmly on what *we* need to be doing differently. The more we do this, the fewer rules we will need for our pupils because they will be more motivated to try to do the right thing.

Here are a few examples of rules we can make for ourselves that will soon become routines:

- Every week learn the names of more and more pupils at your school, not just the ones in your year, so that as you pass pupils in the corridor or on the playground you can greet them by name and with a smile. This has two beneficial results:
  - Each of the pupils you greet by name will feel a bit more cared about, more a part of the school community, and therefore more motivated to follow the community's routines.
  - Each one whose name you clearly remember will feel more visible, more accountable. We all know that there is less crime, proportionally, in a village than in a city. One of the reasons for this is the visibility inherent in a small community, which makes people more aware of others' reactions and therefore more careful. But in the relative

anonymity of a large group, it can be all too easy to "get away with" unacceptable behaviour.

This is especially true in large comprehensives, where teachers report that *they* feel invisible, outnumbered and ineffective, especially in the corridors and playgrounds. The more teachers in your school are willing to take on this new routine as a project, the sooner you can reclaim for civilisation the public parts of the school.

- Never do for a pupil what he is capable of doing for himself. This also means not doing the *thinking* for our pupils and includes:
    - not accepting "I don't know"
    - teaching pupils to answer their own questions
    - not accepting blanks or missed-out answers on written work.

(Chapter 6, on self-reliance, goes into great detail about how to get our pupils into the habit of thinking for themselves.)

- In the classroom, only talk to pupils when they are in the right place. Obviously, this will cut down on telling off from the teachers, but more surprisingly, it will also cut down on pupils wandering around. Telling and retelling is the least effective way to change our pupils' habits. If you are wondering how you can possibly get a pupil back to his seat without talking to him, read on. In this chapter, I will discuss how we can make our rules and routines stick.

- Both in their speaking and in their writing, always require full sentences from our pupils, unless we specifically ask for one-word answers. It is almost impossible for pupils with special educational needs to learn to write clearly and correctly if they have not learned to speak clearly and correctly. This habit will help them improve both spoken and written communication. I discuss this more in the companion volume "Learning to Listen, Listening to Learn", which is all about our language and our pupils' language.

- Here is an alternative to criticism when you see pupils slouching, avoiding eye-contact, fiddling, doodling, whispering, etc, that whole host of very minor but eventually irritating off-task behaviours. Saying loudly, "Head up, hands down" is a much more positive way of reminding them to do the right thing. Of course, as soon as you see even a slight improvement, you have to show that you are pleased. (Chapter 4, on Descriptive Praise, gives many examples of how we can do this.)

2. How to establish rules and routines

It is not enough to teach pupils *how* to follow instructions, be polite, answer in complete sentences, etc. We must also train pupils rigorously and consistently so that they habitually and automatically follow the guidelines, rules and routines that the adults have decided upon.

Establish policies and routines that address the typical issues that arise in your classroom. Children and teenagers are often very predictable in their responses to situations; therefore, it is usually quite easy to identify, in advance, almost all the areas that may present problems.

Take the time to go over policies and rules *before* problems occur. Make your expectations clear. Check that your pupils understand what your expectations are by asking them to describe them in their own words. Take whatever time is necessary to discuss why certain regulations exist. While you may think that pupils should know the reasons for rules without needing any discussion, this is not always the case.

Establishing routines saves time, energy, hassle, and confusion in the long run, but it does require planning to be effective. Make sure that each part of the day has a firm structure, so that your pupils know exactly what is expected of them at all times. Eliminating opportunities for misbehaviour will make it much easier for the disruptive pupils to do the right thing.

For example, have the pupils always:
- line up in order
- enter the classroom silently
- do specified activities at the beginning and end of each lesson and transitions.

Tell the pupils (and then follow through and show them) that there will be positive consequences (rewards) for positive behaviour as well as negative consequences (which used to be called punishments) for negative behaviour. There need to be more rewards than punishments so that all pupils can see that it is easy to earn rewards. Even small rewards are highly motivating because they are symbols of appreciation and approval, which is the reward that every single one of us craves and deserves.

To prevent a lot of rule-breaking and rule-bending, there need to be *frequent* whole-class discussions. The aim is for pupils to know the rules, policies, guidelines, and routines so well that they can explain them to you thoroughly, including the reasons for the rules, with absolutely no prompting. And do not accept vague statements like, "We should be good" or "So we'll learn better". Also, pupils need to know *exactly* what will happen when they behave appropriately, co-operate, and do their best, and exactly what will happen when they don't.

During these discussions:
- Keep the emphasis on positive behaviour and rewards.
- Make sure that you are asking the questions and the pupils are doing the talking. They will listen to themselves and to each other much more carefully than they will listen to a teacher.

Practise every detail of every routine many times out of context (before the need for it) so that you can be (almost) certain of pupils remembering to do it when the need arises. Leave nothing to chance. Leave nothing unpractised. Assume nothing.

When your class contains one or more pupils who are often either angry or impulsive, make sure that you re-establish the rules for conduct and academic work at the beginning of each lesson. These rules and guidelines will need to be reviewed several times within every lesson, if the problem is serious and persistent. These rules should cover all problem areas, such as: acceptable language, behaviour during the lesson, behaviour in the corridors and playground, acceptable and unacceptable reactions to boredom, stress or frustration, first things to do upon entering the classroom, etc.

Do not put your list of rules up on the wall. This may seem like strange advice. I say this because the list will soon blend into the background, and pupils will no longer notice it. This undermines the importance that the rules should be given.

Any well-run classroom needs dozens of rules and routines, far more than you can get on to a list. Plus you want to retain the freedom and flexibility to change rules and routines as you see fit. However, think carefully before you make changes or you will confuse the very pupils who most need stability and structure.

Here are some positive behaviours that we want to see more of in our classrooms. A teacher might easily overlook these because it seems as if they are no more than what we have a right to expect from pupils:

- homework in on time
- homework in late but at least it's in
- working quietly
- raising his hand and waiting to be called on, rather than blurting out or interrupting
- good attendance
- keeping his desk uncluttered
- smiling
- wearing the correct uniform
- contributing to class discussions
- helping a classmate
- not laughing at a classmate's mistake
- answering in a full sentence
- promptly following instructions
- answering his own questions, using common sense
- keeping his hair out of his eyes.

Here is another old proverb, "You can lead a horse to water but you can't make him drink.". Farmers know that you can, however, motivate the horse to *want* to drink, by salting the oats – in other words, by arranging matters so that the horse is thirsty! We can use a similar approach with pupils. They will be motivated to improve their behaviour and academic performance when they see that praise and rewards soon follow.

Pupils will not think you are being "too strict" and will not resent your firm decision-making and follow-through as long as you remember to smile more, criticise less, and Descriptively Praise frequently.

Before a problem arises, establish the consequences for compliance and non-compliance with instructions, routines or rules. You are more likely to follow through with a consequence if you have planned what it should be. When a pupil knows what the consequences will be, he gradually becomes responsible for his own behaviour by "choosing" between the consequences for compliance and the consequences for non-compliance.

Requests for exceptions can be met with a simple look. This should not be a look of annoyance, but an amused, friendly look conveying your surprise that once-established rules are being questioned, or that once-discussed reasons have been forgotten. When pupils ask for special concessions of any kind, your standard answer could be something like: "Not this time. I'll think about it and if I decide that it's a good idea, you can *earn* the privilege for a future time.".

Whenever possible, give pupils choices so that they develop self-reliance, common sense and skill at prioritising. When pupils are consistently given choices it takes some of the sting out of always having to follow orders and do things someone else's way. When giving choices:

- Before you even start talking, be absolutely sure within yourself that you will be completely comfortable with whichever option the pupil chooses.
- Present only two options to choose from.
- Don't make life more complicated for yourself. The choices that you present should simplify matters, not require that you spend more time monitoring or keeping extensive records.
- If pupils do not choose quickly, you decide for them in order to discourage time-wasting.
- Once a pupil has chosen an option, hold him to it. Do not let him change his mind. Over time, this will help him to learn to think before he speaks.

Insist on a realistic but challenging academic standard, in terms of accuracy, thoroughness and presentation.

3. How to follow through

We often hear that consequences, both for positive and negative behaviour, need to be immediate and consistent in order for the most difficult pupils to be sufficiently motivated to modify their behaviour. Although that makes obvious sense, it is *much* easier said than done. Many teachers find the whole area of follow-through fraught with problems. I shall attempt to clarify just how we can give immediate and consistent consequences.

3a. Following through after positive behaviour

If we wait until pupils do something very good before we reward them, then the very pupils who most need those boosts to their self-esteem will rarely "deserve" rewards. So we need to be very generous with our rewards, noticing and responding to all the little steps in the right direction.

Here are some examples of small, easy rewards that you can give frequently. You will see that some will be most effective with a specific age group, while others are universal.

- Smiles and Descriptive Praise. This is the easiest, quickest and most appreciated reward. (See Chapter 4.)
- More choices (e.g. where to sit in the classroom, which activity to do next, how many sums to do).
- The chance to play a "learning game" for five minutes at the end of the lesson.
- A night free of homework.
- A note or phone call to parents.
- The pupil's name on a special chart.
- The chance to help the teacher.
- Being given extra responsibilities.
- Being the first in line or the first to do something fun.
- A five-minute chat with the teacher at break-time.
- The chance to run an errand for the teacher.
- Ticks or points.
- Five minutes of drawing at the end of the lesson.

- A slightly longer break.
- A short movement activity.

Notice that we are not talking about any rewards that cost money or that pupils can lose, fiddle with, shred, scatter or steal from each other.

There will be many times when you give a pupil a little reward (e.g. Descriptive Praise) for even beginning a task. Our aim is to establish the HABIT of co-operation. Standards can be raised once the HABIT of actually doing what he has been told has been established.

3b. Following through after negative behaviour

You may hear people making a distinction between "consequences" and "punishment". Nowadays, the word "punishment" has fallen out of favour and is often applied to any method of reacting to misbehaviour which:

- is arbitrary or barely related to the logic of the situation
- implies moral judgement or moral superiority
- is concerned only with past behaviour rather than with helping the pupil to improve from now on
- is carried out in anger
- is disrespectful of the wrongdoer's feelings or motives.

Obviously, we want to avoid all the above, both when we talk about misbehaviour and when we follow through after misbehaviour has occurred.

Negative behaviour falls into two categories:
- Definite infractions of a rule, which can be:
    - minor or major
    - impulsive, compulsive, deliberate or habitual
- Subtle "bending" of a rule or of an implicit expectation.

To earn the respect of the pupils, we need to respond immediately to all these kinds of negative behaviour positively, firmly and consistently. This is how we will nip the negative behaviour in the bud and establish a classroom atmosphere that is calm, friendly and focused. It is easy, however, in the interests of "delivering the curriculum", to let small bits of non-co-operation slip through the net. After all, they're so small. It can be very tempting to be inconsistent about follow-through. When faced with a non-stop stream of minor misbehaviour it is easy to under-react, by ignoring, or to over-react, by telling off or warning. These habitual ways of responding are simply not effective at reducing the frequency, duration or intensity of impulsive, compulsive, habitual or deliberate misbehaviour:

- seeming not to notice the problem behaviour
- giving the pupil another chance before he has earned it by appropriate behaviour
- giving a reprimand (which is generally worse then useless) instead of taking action.

Why aren't we more consistent about consequences?

- We get tired, fed up, frustrated by dealing with the same misbehaviour again and again. We think, "What's the use?".
- We may not be sure that we can control our own anger.
- We do not want to provoke further resentment and misbehaviour.
- We may not feel supported by our senior management team.
- If other teachers at our school are not consistent, we are reluctant to seem like the only "bad guy".

Most misbehaviour is minor and more likely to be impulsive, compulsive or habitual rather than deliberate. How we respond to this minor misbehaviour will have a huge influence on the atmosphere in our classroom. The calmer and more positive we can stay, the calmer and more positive our pupils will become, and much sooner than we imagine.

In addition, how we respond to minor misbehaviour will determine, to a large extent, how little or how much *major* misbehaviour we are faced with. When we do not deal *effectively* with the little problems, not only do we get more of them, but also unintentionally we send out a signal of weakness. Some pupils will react by thinking, "Let's see what else I can get away with.". So it is in our interest to become familiar with and to consistently apply the tried and tested techniques that have been proven to reduce teacher-pupil conflicts and improve the optimism and focus of everyone involved.

My advice is to overlook nothing. Always follow through, even on very minor infractions, so that your pupils realise that there is no point in testing. They should know from observation and from personal experience what will happen! Only give a second chance after a pupil has earned it by a period of good behaviour.

When a pupil is misbehaving or not working properly, in our frustration we sometimes find ourselves saying completely useless things that make us cringe when we think about it afterwards. As soon as we utter the comment, we realise that we missed an opportunity to motivate, teach, show respect or compassion. Teachers are very caring, dedicated professionals, so when this happens we tend to blame and berate ourselves. We wonder if we are cut out for the job or if we are just too negative, or too weak, or too angry, or too idealistic.

We may find ourselves responding to minor off-task behaviour or rule-breaking with repetitive comments such as:

- Get to work, please.
- Look at me when I'm talking to you.
- Everyone's almost finished, and you've barely started.
- Don't just sit there.
- What are you doing?
- Don't just guess; think!
- We're not interested in that right now.
- Leave that alone.
- You're not paying attention.
- Will you be quiet, please.
- Stop bothering him.
- You're very distractible today.
- Stop fidgeting.

Don't fall into the trap of thinking – or hoping – that a reprimand is enough of a consequence. Many disruptive pupils expect reprimands, and take them in their stride; reprimands are not effective consequences. Nothing you *say* will convince a pupil that you mean business: you must take action.

Also, do not make the typical adult mistake of assuming that children and teenagers actually listen to our articulate, well-reasoned, logical advice! Mostly, young people tune out anything that sounds to them even remotely like criticism. Whenever you are tempted to remind or moralise or give advice, bite your tongue and Descriptively Praise instead. Later, when you are alone or brainstorming with a colleague, decide on a policy, plan or routine that you can establish to achieve the result you want. This is far more effective than trying to convince pupils to follow your advice.

Do not negotiate or compromise on anything that you feel is right. You, the adult, may not be perfect or know all the answers, but you definitely have much more experience, maturity and wisdom than your pupils do. If you think you are right about something but are not sure, take heart: you probably are right. So start out by assuming that you are right. You can doubt yourself after 4 p.m., but while at school, speak and act with conviction, as if you are so convinced you are right that you are not even tempted to argue, plead, bribe, threaten, preach or give up!

Stop everything as soon as unacceptable behaviour occurs! If you are not sure what to do next, buy some time by being silent and just looking at the pupil.

When a pupil does not follow an instruction right away, do not assume that he will continue to refuse. Do not give up. Keep waiting. Keep Descriptively Praising every step in the right direction, or even the absence of the wrong thing. For example, if you have just asked a pupil to stand up, and he is not doing it, you could say, "You're not arguing with me right now; thank you.".

A pupil's inappropriate behaviour is reinforced when he gets attention for it. Therefore, do not make a fuss, get upset, or sound annoyed, but do not ignore inappropriate behaviour. There are other, calmer ways of letting the pupil know that you see exactly what he is doing and that there is a consequence.

Here are some helpful responses to minor misbehaviour. First of all, do not repeat the instructions or rules or expectations. If pupils continue to

do something they have been told not to do (or they continue not to do something they have been told to do), instead of repeating your original instruction, do one of the following:

- Just moving closer to the pupil who is causing a problem often serves to remind him to get back on-task.
- Point to a place (e.g. on the whiteboard) where you have written down the instruction or rule.
- Descriptively Praise those who are behaving appropriately, and the others will soon want to imitate. Make sure to Descriptively Praise the late-behavers too as soon as they comply, so that they learn that imitating good behaviour is rewarded.
- Ask other pupils what is needed. This helps pupils to start seeing themselves through others' eyes.
- Stop everything and look at the child pointedly (not with an annoyed expression on your face) and wait for him to figure out why. Silence and a prolonged look will make a pupil aware that he is doing something inappropriate. A look is far more effective, especially in the long run, than an explanation, an argument, a sarcastic remark, or a repeated request. This gentle way of guiding a pupil back to acceptable behaviour is especially effective if rules have *already* been established regarding acceptable and unacceptable behaviour.

  A look (continued until the pupil is on-task again) is more effective, because:

  - children and teenagers tend to tune out anything that sounds like criticism
  - words interrupt the flow of the lesson
  - words draw attention to the problem, and we want to draw attention to things working smoothly so that co-operation seems to the pupils to be the normal state of affairs in each classroom.

- Paradoxically, even a smile will often work to bring a pupil back to more appropriate behaviour.
- Interestingly, Descriptive Praise is very effective at getting a pupil to behave appropriately. It means you have to think fast to

come up with something to Descriptively Praise, just at the moment when you feel like reprimanding.

- You can deprive a disruptive pupil of the "rewards" of attention-seeking by removing him from the limelight. Put the pupil in a quiet place and tell him to stay there as long as he needs to in order to settle down and get ready to work. Giving the pupil permission to stay isolated from the group is likely to make him want to rejoin the group as soon as possible. Make him wait until you can *see* that he is ready to co-operate, rather than taking his word for it.

Do not repeat, remind, scold, preach, apologise, persuade, justify, explain, etc. The pupils have heard it all before! If these tactics have not worked thus far, why expect them to miraculously work this time? Don't say: "John, how many times do I have to tell you? Hang up your coat on the hook before you sit down.". Instead, prepare for sucess. Before pupils enter the room, ask them, "What will you do before you sit down?".

And then Descriptively Praise a pupil who is doing it right. As pupils enter the classroom say, loud enough for John to hear, "Amy, you remembered to hang your coat up on the hook before you sat down".

If John has still not hung up his coat by the time everyone is seated, say to the class, "Almost everyone remembered to hang up their coat on the hook before they sat down.". You may need to be standing very close to John when you say this, so that you get his attention. And when John does take the hint and rouse himself to do the right thing, resist the temptation to roll your eyes and say "Finally!" Instead, Descriptively Praise: "Thank you for remembering, John.".

You may be feeling by now that it would be much easier to just tell John to hang up his coat. But remember that our aim is not just to get the coat hung up. Even more important is getting our pupils into the habit of telling themselves the right thing to do.

What has been proven to help pupils learn to control their impulsivity and motivate them to change their habits is a technique called the Action Replay. This consists of having the pupil do the action again, but this time he does it right. If he just grabbed something, during the Action Replay he will wait, say "please", take the item without snatching and then say "thank you". If he pushed past someone, have him say "excuse me" and wait. If he swore, have him say how he feels without swearing. When a pupil complains, have him make a polite request. When he interrupts, replay the scene, and this time he has to wait until the other person stops talking. When he does sloppy work, have him re-do it. And of course be very pleased when he does it right. Once you start using Action Replays you will see that they are very effective at re-training habits.

At first, you will find yourself using Action Replays 10, 20, even 30 times a day. Each one only takes a few minutes, and benefits the rest of the class as well. They will be watching and listening, learning from the Action Replay that you mean what you say, that you are consistent, that you are confident that each pupil is capable of doing the right thing and that it is never too late to right a wrong. Action Replays "wipe the slate clean".

Teachers are always very pleasantly surprised at how willing even resistant, disruptive pupils are to do Action Replays. Remember that most minor misbehaviour is impulsive, compulsive or habitual (rather than deliberate), so as long as we stay positive and calm, pupils generally like the idea of doing it the right way and receiving Descriptive Praise.

Two questions always crop up when teachers are contemplating incorporating Action Replays into their classroom routines:
- What if the pupil point-blank refuses to do the Action Replay?
- What if he is willing to do the Action Replay, but he doesn't take it seriously, doesn't try to do it properly, or tries to make a fool of me?

My reply:

Both of these situations will occur very occasionally, especially in the first few weeks, while your pupils are still testing your consistency.

Whether it is outright refusal or more subtle testing, do not give up. Just say, "I can see you're not ready to do the Action Replay just yet. I'll come back in a few minutes.". Continue teaching, and in a few minutes, go

back to the pupil and say, "Are you ready to do the Action Replay yet?".
Eventually, and usually sooner rather than later, the pupil will realise that
a) you are not going to forget about this and b) you are not angry. It
becomes easier, and more appealing, to do the Action Replay than to
resist, either actively or passively. You might think that a typical teenager
would hate the idea of an Action Replay and see it as losing face or
giving in. However, staying calm and friendly takes the sting out of it, so
that it is not experienced as humiliation or punishment, simply as
practice at doing things the right way.

Do not give a pupil a second chance until he has earned it by doing an
Action Replay and meeting specific behaviour standards for a specific
length of time.

Of course, when the pupil stops the problem behaviour or completes the
Action Replay, smile at him and give him a small nod of approval or the
"thumbs up" sign or a quick Descriptive Praise.

Sometimes you will experience an epidemic of minor misbehaviour, a
wave of off-task behaviour, aimless chatter, shouting out and complaints
that sweeps over your classroom. Rather than trying to deal with each
incident separately, work on changing the atmosphere in a more global
way. Requiring five minutes of silence is an excellent way to calm down a
class; so is reading aloud to them, telling them a story or recounting a
happy or successful experience you all had together, such as a class play or
a museum trip.

Interestingly, a short consequence is often more effective than a long one.
A short consequence engenders less resentment and gets the pupil back
sooner to the happy state of earning rewards. Also, there is less chance
that a teacher will forget the consequence, find it inconvenient, take pity
on the pupil or give in.

A consequence should be uncomfortable enough to get the pupil's
attention, but not so upsetting that it breeds more resentment.

As tempting as it might be, do not protect the pupil from the
consequences of his action or lack of action. When we are inconsistent,
pupils stop taking us seriously.

One purpose of a consequence is to prompt the pupil to think to himself: "I wish I hadn't done that! I guess I'd better be more careful next time, so that I won't have to miss break time (or work when the others are playing, or sit silently at my desk for 15 minutes, etc)". The pupil will only be prompted to think this if we are consistent.

One effective consequence is that the pupil is not allowed to do anything fun until he has complied with your instruction. This might mean sitting in silence while the others move on to the next activity or missing break or playtime. I do not recommend doing this frequently because the very pupil who is likely to be kept in is usually the kinesthetic type whose behaviour deteriorates rapidly if he does not have a chance to move and let off steam. Examples of appropriate consequences for minor negative behaviour:
- Action Replays
- staying after the lesson
- a shorter break
- not having earned the right to make choices
- sitting near the teacher
- not having earned a privilege or reward
- sitting apart from a friend.

As much as possible, it is a good idea for the consequences of minor negative behaviour to take place in your classroom. Pupils lose respect for the teacher who frequently sends pupils to the head or who gives lots of detentions because it leaves the impression that the teacher is not able to handle the disruptive behaviour. Also, immediate consequences are usually far more effective than delayed consequences. An exception is the pupil who rarely gets into trouble; he is likely to be suitably impressed by a visit to the head or a detention, although he probably will not need that to help him get back on track.

Extra homework should never he given as a consequence because:
- pupils who already hate and avoid homework will not learn anything constructive from it, even if they do it
- as it is not an in-school consequence, it cannot be monitored, and even more problems are created if the homework is not done, or not done properly.

A teacher may worry that insisting by waiting and Descriptively Praising will provoke an angry pupil to further misbehaviour or even to violence. Of course, I cannot guarantee that this will not happen, but my own experience and all the reports I have received from teachers tells me that the very opposite is usually true. What is likely to infuriate an already resentful pupil is lecturing, criticising, threatening or shouting. Descriptive Praise, a "long fuse" and smiling usually calm things down very quickly. You might not be ready to believe me if you have had some unpleasant encounters, where you felt intimidated or even scared for your safety. I am certainly not suggesting that you take any risks with your safety. I think that Descriptive Praise, Reflective Listening, showing that you are the "captain" of your classroom and all the other techniques in this book are your best bets for creating and maintaining peace and order.

Unfortunately, we are not only faced with *minor* misbehaviour. Sometimes following-through means taking action on a bigger scale. Nowadays all schools have a Behaviour Policy that lays out the consequences for *major* misbehaviour. I suggest that you always follow that policy, even if you are concerned that:

- it might not do any good so it would just be a waste of time and effort
- other teachers or the senior management team might think you can't cope
- the senior management team will not support you if the parents complain.

Let's say that the pupil had to be excluded. When he comes back into your class, do not act as if nothing has happened. If, out of kindness, you ignore the pupil's past rule-breaking, unfortunately it will be interpreted by some pupils as weakness, fear and appeasement. To show that you are the "captain" of your classroom, I advise you to openly welcome him back and take the time, in front of his classmates as well as one-to-one, to Descriptively Praise him for any little improvement. This may not feel comfortable, either for you or for that pupil, but it reinforces the stand you have taken about appropriate behaviour.

If it feels to you as if there would be just too many times in a day when your pupils would get to the point of non-compliance, you may be falling into the trap of:

- giving too many instructions
- not preparing for success with frequent discussions of expectations and consequences
- not Descriptively Praising enough.

When the same pupil keeps getting consequences, this should warn us that the consequences are not working to reduce the misbehaviour. Consequences are not magic. They are only one component of a behaviour improvement plan that should also include successful academic experiences and lots of appreciation.

Chapter 6
Fostering self-reliance

1. What we mean by self-reliance

As important as it is (for obvious reasons) for our pupils to get into the habit of following a teacher's instructions immediately, there is another habit that is, ultimately, even more important for pupils to develop. This is the habit of using their own common sense, the habit of taking responsibility for their actions. This habit is what we call self-reliance.

It also goes by other names:
- thinking for oneself
- doing one's best
- using one's initiative
- self-discipline.

At its most basic, self-reliance means telling oneself the right thing to do and then doing it, instead of expecting or hoping or waiting for someone else to remind you or motivate you or give in and do it for you.

Once a pupil has demonstrated that he *can* do something, from that moment on, our job is to train the pupil in the habit of reminding himself to do it. So resist the temptation to tell him what to do or how to do it.

2. What we *are* doing when we are not actively training our pupils in self-reliance

We may explain and then re-explain, and then tell and prompt and remind some more. This leaves the teacher frustrated and the pupil resentful. And meanwhile the pupil is not learning to take responsibility for his memory or his actions.

We may find ourselves criticising, lecturing, moralising and predicting a dire future.

We may, in our frustration, resort to shouting, sarcasm, threats and multiple warnings.

We may get so fed up with re-telling, day after day, and week after week, that we gradually mention our expectations less and less. We either hope that pupils will remember and comply or we despair of their ever remembering and complying consistently. We may even vacillate between hope and despair. Either way, the responsibility for getting themselves into good habits is being left up to the pupils. And as we have seen, only a tiny minority, the "easiest" or most mature, is able to train themselves.

3. Why it is important for teachers to take on the job of training pupils to become self-reliant

Self-reliance leads to self-confidence. The more thinking a pupil does for himself, the sooner he will develop confidence in his ability to handle the inevitable problems that will crop up in his life.

As we saw in Chapter 2, pupils with learning difficulties, attention problems or disruptive, disrespectful behaviour are often suffering from immature or impaired auditory processing. These pupils have a much harder time than most doing the following:

- paying attention to auditory stimuli
    - partly because they are so easily distracted by background stimuli, both visual and auditory
    - partly because they have a greater than average inborn urge to move around, which in itself distracts them from steady focusing
- "translating" what they hear into mental pictures
- remembering what they hear
- realising the importance of what they hear.

Because of these problems, teachers often find themselves reminding these pupils to pay attention or finish their work or stop wasting time. It is very tempting for teachers to remind, explain, justify, sometimes even cajole, bribe, threaten, criticise or shout.

However, the more often a teacher reminds and gives the same instructions day after day, the more likely these pupils are to switch off and tune out. This, understandably, leads the teacher to prompt and remind even more and to become, over time, louder, shriller and more and more annoyed-sounding. Yet these pupils still manage not to pay much attention to our instructions! The good news is that getting pupils to *tell themselves* what to do has been shown to result in pupils doing what they are supposed to be doing far more of the time.

The more often that you find yourself, day after day, giving the same kinds of instructions, reminders and prompts, the more exasperated and frustrated you are bound to become over time (unless you are a saint). This significantly affects your degree of job satisfaction. It's no fun beating your head against a brick wall.

Pupils gradually lose respect for teachers who remind, cajole, plead and get annoyed. Pupils stop even trying to please these teachers. They may even go out of their way to provoke and upset the teachers who always seem to be talking about what pupils are doing wrong.

Interestingly, pupils use the term "strict" when describing teachers who talk a lot about misbehaviour and seem annoyed or distant, even though these teachers may not be strict in the sense of consistent. When teachers become more consistent, they are seen as "nice" and "friendly" and "understanding", even though they are actually stricter.

Some pupils seem to pick up new skills, facts and ideas easily, seemingly by osmosis. By and large, these are the pupils who are "good at" listening, observing and making connections. These pupils delight us with their blossoming self-reliance and self-confidence.

But the pupils who typically cause problems for us, for their peers and for themselves rarely fall into this category. In particular, those with auditory processing weaknesses show us, time and again, that they need our input more than the other pupils do. The truth of the following sentence is obvious: "Teaching requires the presence of the teacher.". It is easy to forget that the following is also true: "Training requires the presence of the trainer.". Sometimes we fall into the trap of assuming that once a pupil has been taught how to do something, we can swiftly move on and teach him the next thing. But for a number of pupils that does not work. Teaching is not enough. We cannot assume that what has been taught will automatically become a habit. We must undertake to help them turn skills into habits; otherwise such a pupil will still "need" reminding (about lining up, about full stops and capitals, about not interrupting, etc.) a full decade after he was first taught the skill.

By presence, I do not of course mean a passive or reactive presence. An active, pro-active presence includes:
- close, frequent supervision
- constructive, consistent feedback.

4. How we can help our pupils to become more self-reliant

a. First we teach

Even pupils with significant learning, attention or behaviour problems can learn and be more successful. But they will need more help from us and in particular a different kind of help.

Often these pupils learn much more slowly (for a variety of reasons) so they will need:
- Much more frequent feedback.
- More time to take in and think about information.
- More time to express themselves, in speaking as well as writing.
- More time with a teacher who understands the necessity of training as well as teaching.
- More time at each stage of learning.
- More practice (especially practice at noticing and evaluating their own work).
- A calmer, quieter, more orderly environment.
- Skilled, experienced adults.
- Supplementary or substitute materials, equipment and activities.

First we need to teach a pupil how to do an action, skill or task, and only then can we train him to do it regularly and automatically, so that he will not need our reminders or prompts. (If you are sure that your pupil knows *how* to do something, you can proceed to train him to do it without being told. See page 83.)

Every task is made up of many much smaller micro-skills.

For example, there are at least 17 micro-skills needed to do a long multiplication sum. Some of the most obvious micro-skills are:

- memorising the multiplication facts so that "head space" is freed up to think about doing the steps in the right order
- putting the "carry" numbers in the right place
- indenting or putting a "nought to hold the place"
- adding (not multiplying) the carry numbers
- accurate addition.

A few of the micro-skills needed to become a successful reader are:

- knowing the sounds of all the letters, blends and diagraphs
- using punctuation to aid understanding
- having a steadily growing stream of sight words.

Some of the micro-skills that make up "co-operation" are:

- staying seated
- raising hands
- only talking about the work
- pitching in when it is time to clean up
- following instructions without a fuss.

Some micro-skills involved in being "friendly" are:

- eye contact
- greeting and returning greetings
- taking turns
- listening instead of interrupting
- responding to what is said, instead of talking only about what one finds interesting.

A common mistake is trying to help a pupil who is confused about something by re-teaching him at the same level as the first explanation. If the pupil is not able to do a task, first we need to teach him the relevant micro-skills. Break each task down into small steps. Reward successful completion of each step with Descriptive Praise.

Sometimes you must do something for a pupil because the task has to get done but he does not yet have the skill to do it. These are usually practical skills, such as tying laces, underlining, and cutting. Rather than simply doing it for the pupil, every single time make the pupil watch and explain to you step by step what you are doing and how and why. That will bring him another small step closer to eventually not needing you.

There will probably be some bits of the task that the pupil can do for himself. Require him to do those by himself, even if you still need to help or remind about other bits of the task. For example, for a pupil who cannot yet use a ruler properly, the teacher can hold the ruler as the pupil runs the pencil along the side of the ruler. You might even need to place your pupil's hand on the ruler in the correct position and then put your hands on top of the pupil's hands to keep them in the correct position and to guide his movements.

If you find yourself explaining a lot or urging and encouraging a lot, you are probably trying to teach too many steps at one time. If you thoroughly teach and revise the micro-skills, you will not have many problems teaching the next skill because the pupil will be and will feel ready for the next step.

Don't rush! Teach each step or micro-skill separately until it is mastered before attempting to combine steps.

Fade out your prompts as soon as possible. For example, instead of telling what the next step is, you can make a gesture or just point.

Each time you attempt to teach, always start at the beginning or with a very easy step. Teach from what the pupil has demonstrated he can do well. Never assume that he can do something well without proof. This will build the pupil's confidence because success breeds success. It will also enable you to see clearly where the difficulties begin to occur.

Explain to the pupil why you are starting at such an easy stage. That way he will not assume that you believe that the easy stage is all he is capable of. He still may not like it. As we know, the pupil with problems is often extremely sensitive. He has been criticised so much that he imagines he is being criticised even when he isn't. Make sure that your pupil understands and can articulate your reasons for teaching him in this way, even though he may resist.

Almost all difficult or unmotivated pupils have a reading comprehension level significantly below the level used in the textbooks for the year they are in. This means that they are spending much of their school day confused or spaced out, frustrated, not really understanding what they are reading or what they are supposed to be doing or why. They soon become used to being confused and just drift through their days, not really expecting their schoolwork to be enjoyable or rewarding. These pupils should be working from much simpler reading material, not only for the sake of their learning and their self-esteem, but also for the sake of their classmates, who often end up bearing the brunt of the frustration.

A quick and very accurate method for judging whether a pupil can cope with the reading comprehension level of a given textbook is to have the pupil put in his own words, sentence by sentence, a paragraph from the textbook, and then have him summarise that paragraph. This will reveal a great deal.

Breaking down skills is particularly necessary for teaching reading comprehension. Many pupils who manage to achieve acceptable scores on standardised reading tests are at a loss when dealing with their textbooks. This is because many standardised tests and other multiple-choice tests do not adequately measure some of the most important components of reading comprehension:

- using contextual clues to understand unfamiliar words
- understanding formal language usage
- understanding complex sentence structure
- drawing inferences
- reaching conclusions
- classifying

- sequencing and prioritising
- paraphrasing
- summarising
- defining and describing
- evaluating information.

All classwork, homework and revision must be at a skill level that is comfortable for the pupil. Require mastery of each step or level before proceeding to the next harder phase.

The teacher's emphasis should always be on assigning work that the pupil can do easily, and requiring it to be done extremely well (which means accurately, thoroughly and neatly) rather than setting work that is too difficult and then accepting a mediocre standard.

Implementing this policy consistently will train pupils to:

- slow down and pay attention
- take each piece of work seriously
- notice their own strengths and weaknesses
- evaluate and revise their work (sometimes several times!)
- sharpen their proofreading skills
- become skilled at paraphrasing and summarising
- actually learn whatever there is to learn from each piece of work
- develop critical thinking.

Class participation can and should be taught and trained. When pupils contribute frequently to class discussions, there are many benefits:

- The pupils are improving their language skills.
- They are becoming more self-confident.
- They are paying attention more and therefore understanding and remembering more.
- An interested, co-operative atmosphere is developing.
- The teacher can measure all the stages of learning: motivation, understanding, retention and use.

There are many techniques that teachers can use to improve the quantity and quality of class participation. One easy way to train pupils to participate in class is to ask an easy question, have all the pupils write down their answers in complete sentences, and then call on each of them to read out their sentences. This method reduces the typical reluctance, hesitation and embarrassment that comes from having to think and talk at the same time. Done daily, this exercise will break down barriers of passivity or nervousness within a few weeks.

To motivate a pupil to keep trying to learn something that feels difficult, remember to use lots of Descriptive Praise (See Chapter 4).

We cannot expect our pupils to be able to read our minds and to know exactly what we want done and how we want it to be done. Be patient while you teach or train; it is worth it in the end.

For example, instead of telling pupils again and again that they should begin revising weeks before an exam rather than cramming and panicking two nights before, take action. For at least a month before the exam, assign some homework or classwork every day that requires the pupil to revise (e.g., memorising terminology, outlining a chapter, summarising important ideas, answering mock-exam questions).

DO NOT RUSH. Rushing is a false economy. We save a few minutes today but store up very time-consuming trouble for ourselves in the days, weeks, months and even years to come.

If a pupil is feeling so unsure of himself that he is not willing to try, this may mean that:

- the relevant micro-skills have not yet been mastered
- your explanation was too quick or sketchy for this pupil
- the pupil is used to getting attention for non-compliance or for learned helplessness rather than for doing things right
- the pupil has often been criticised for getting things wrong and has, therefore, developed a mental block. This pupil may come across as stubborn, silly, paralysed, tired, anxious, day-dreamy, easily distracted, bored, or disruptive. Underneath all this negative behaviour this pupil is probably feeling afraid or angry or both.

b. Then we train

We have already seen, in Chapter 3, that when pupils respect a teacher, motivation for the difficult task of learning new habits grows steadily.

In Chapter 4, we saw that when we appreciate every tiny step in the right direction, we get more and more of those tiny steps.

And Chapter 5 talked about how motivation increases when we take the time to make it absolutely clear to our pupils what they should do and not do. The more we put into practice the tools from these chapters, the easier it will be for our pupils to become self-reliant, focused, resourceful, confident learners.

We need to constantly review previously learned skills and information so that the pupil's responses become habitual and automatic. Schedule in repetition and practice in a variety of circumstances so that pupils develop the habit of transferring skills to new situations.

Our aim is to achieve over-learning by teaching, re-teaching and providing so much practice at every step along the way that the pupil thoroughly understands, remembers and feels confident with the material. Over-learning enables the pupils to articulate concepts, carry out procedures correctly and transfer knowledge and skills to unfamiliar situations, even under adverse circumstances. This means that a large percentage of the skill, habit or information remains, even when the pupil is:

- unsupervised
- tired
- not well
- anxious
- resentful
- rushing
- preoccupied
- uninterested
- hungry
- upset
- distracted.

Over-learning must be specifically built into the lessons. Drills in game form lessen the potential monotony of straightforward drill. For over-learning to happen, we need to space the repetitions of material over time rather than massing the experiences in a short time span. When a new concept is presented, come back to it again and again, often in new settings, not just as a drill game but as transfer to a new situation.

Getting pupils into the habit of following instructions immediately is an important step towards self-reliance. Once pupils are in the habit of co-operating with our instructions, as long as we keep our routines predictable, soon some pupils will sometimes follow the routines without waiting to be told. The more we notice this and show we are pleased, the more pupils will be motivated to remember and then do the right thing. The trickle becomes a groundswell.

Remember that training a pupil to do something properly or to follow a routine consistently only seems to take more of your time than simply issuing commands would take. If you think that you do not have time to spare for training, just think how much time is already spent (wasted!) on repeating yourself, arguing, cajoling, redoing, nagging, worrying, etc.

Each exercise or activity should be divided into three distinct stages:

Stage One:

A thorough talk-through. The aim in this stage is to prepare pupils to be able to do the work:
- by themselves
- with confidence
- thoroughly and accurately.

Stage Two:

Pupils work independently, with very little help, explanations or reminders from the teacher. This is true self-reliance.

Stage Three:

Pupils examine and improve their work, with input from the teacher and from other pupils.

At first, it might seem that Stage Two is the most important part of the lesson and that the most time should be devoted to that stage. However, the key to successful learning, more positive behaviour and enhanced confidence and self-reliance is a very thorough *talk-through*.

A talk-through is not just the introduction to each new part of the lesson. It is an introduction with a major and significant difference because *you* will not be doing the telling. Your job is to ask lots of questions, and the pupils' job is to remind themselves, problem-solve and say aloud what they will do and how they will do it. The more time you are willing to spend on numerous talk-throughs, several times every day, the more competent, confident and self-reliant your pupils will become, the more smoothly your classroom will run, the more your pupils will learn and the more relaxed you will be.

Examples of talk-through questions:
- Why do you think I have given you this piece of work to do?
- How many sentences do you think will satisfy me?
- Why do spelling, punctuation and handwriting matter, even when the subject is not English?
- What should you do if you don't get the result you expect in your experiment?
- What is the routine I want you to follow if you finish early?
- How can you help each other if someone is feeling stuck?

Make it absolutely clear before pupils begin working which parts of the task they can make their own choices about, and in which they must follow your instructions to the letter. Prevent silly choices by giving limited choices, not open choices, and by being absolutely sure you will be satisfied with whichever of the limited choices a pupil chooses.

Demonstrate to pupils *exactly* how you want work to be done. For example, give the pupil a visual model for the layout and presentation of every piece of work. Do not allow exceptions if you want the pupil to learn to think carefully and proofread carefully.

Always make sure that pupils know why they are doing every piece of work. But don't tell them; ask them to tell you.

Discipline yourself not to answer your pupils' questions. This may seem strange advice because, of course, we want our pupils to be curious and to be concerned, both of which necessitate asking questions. Yes, asking questions can be valuable if it leads to sharper thinking skills and an increased sense of responsibility. But I have seen that teaching pupils to answer their own questions is a more effective way to get them thinking and paying attention and caring and seeing the point of what they are supposed to be doing. Even though the process of drawing a sensible answer from a pupil takes time at first, soon you will see a marked increase in common sense and self-confidence.

Utilise pupils to help explain rules and procedures to other pupils. One way is to pair together old and new pupils or able and less-able pupils. The more experienced one will usually respond with a feeling of pride because he can show the ropes, and the newer one will be grateful for a guide. This can provide you with the time to concentrate on a specific issue or individual.

Even after a thorough talk-through you may find that all is not crystal clear. When a pupil wants your attention for individual help, it is tempting to re-explain. But often that is not what is best for him. Particularly when several pupils are clamouring for your help at the same time, it is especially helpful to remember that although they may want individual attention, they do not necessarily need it at that time. What they probably need most at that moment is to:
  • practise answering their own questions
  • practise bravely tackling work that they feel somewhat unsure of.

After the talk-through, wait for pupils to remember what to do and then to do it. While you are waiting, Descriptively Praise every step in the right direction. Waiting may seem like a passive or insignificant non-action. Actually, waiting is very powerful. Waiting conveys that what you are waiting for them to do is so important that you will not shift your focus onto the next activity until your expectations are met. Waiting conveys that you are requiring compliance, rather than requesting it.

While you are waiting, you will notice some pupils getting on with it and other pupils staring into space, chatting, or carrying on with their previous activity. Resist the urge to remind. Remember that the more you remind the more you will have to remind. Instead, one way to help a pupil remind himself is the technique called "planting a seed": rather than telling, gently steer the pupil's thoughts in the right direction. By bringing a vivid mental picture of the desired behaviour into the forefront of a pupil's mind, we maximise the likelihood that the pupil will remember and will do it.

An example is:

"What learning activity do you plan to choose after you finish your Maths sums?"

That one innocent question is packed with "embedded" reminders. It reminds the pupil, without actually telling him, that:

- he cannot just do whatever he feels like after he finishes his Maths
- he needs to "plan" (i.e. think about and choose in advance) his next activity
- he has choices
- his choices are limited; his next activity has to be a "learning activity"
- that you may check up and see if he does what he says he will do.

In addition, this open-ended and positively phrased question can convey that:

- the teacher assumes that the pupil will finish his Maths in time to do the next activity
- the teacher believes that the pupil is capable of making sensible choices
- the teacher is interested in the pupil.

This last point may seem an odd one to make. Surely our pupils know that we care about them? Smiles, praise and listening are the standard ways of showing that we care. Unless we are doing these things frequently, a pupil may not know that we care.

Other examples of planting a seed:

- "Tell me what you'll be looking for when you re-read your finished essay."
- "Who remembers exactly how we line up?"
- "Put your hand up if you know one of the necessary steps in division of fractions." (Answering this type of question correctly does not require memory of the sequence or even much prior understanding.)
- "What do we all need to do before lunch-time?"
- "I see two tables (or two rows or two pupils or over half the room, etc) who are remembering what to do."

Most teachers report that they already use this type of subtle prompt, most often with their most reliable, most motivated or most able pupils. However, I strongly recommend that you extend your use of this type of prompt to whenever you know a pupil is capable of doing the action, instead of just telling him to get on with it.

Non-verbal prompts are the last stage in between the extreme, on one end of the spectrum, of telling the pupil to do something and, on the other end, requiring the pupil to tell himself and then to do it. A non-verbal prompt might be:

- Point to the object or to the place where the information is.
- Make removable posters that list sequences of events, steps in a task, materials needed etc., so that you can point to them, rather than telling or repeating. The reason for removable posters is that any visual stimulus that is left up will soon become "invisible", like wallpaper.
- Pick up a disorganised, forgetful pupil's homework diary from the floor and put it on his desk so that he is more likely to see it and take it home. Remember to notice when he does take it home, and be sure to remember to give Descriptive Praise.

5. A frequently asked question

"In theory, I see the point of training in self-reliance. But how can I when I don't have the time? The National Curriculum feels like a juggernaut that flattens everything in its path, including all my good intentions."

> My reply:
> "In Chapter 1, I talked about viewing these new techniques as an investment, rather than as a sacrifice. Yes, it takes time to get our pupils into good habits but it takes even more time (not to mention grey hairs) to repeat and remind for weeks and months and even years."

Chapter 7
A new beginning

By the time you reach this final chapter you may have a number of possible reactions. You may be feeling:

- inspired and empowered
- insulted and patronised
- delighted, excited
- discouraged, depressed
- reassured, appreciated
- "These techniques cannot possibly live up to the author's claims."
- "These techniques might work.".

I am hoping that you are saying to yourself, "These techniques might work, so what have I got to lose?".

When you commit to putting these techniques into practice consistently, it can feel very uncomfortable at first:

- You may feel discouraged, worrying that these techniques cannot possibly make enough of a difference.
- It may feel like it is too much of a chore to be so consistent.
- You may be worried that you won't do it well, so you might be reluctant to try it and then fail.
- It may feel as if you do not have the time.
- You may be concerned that you will get confused and forget which skill to use when.

- You may want to protest that your pupils are not typical:
  - they're mostly special needs
  - they're mostly EFL
  - they live on a terribly deprived estate
  - they're stoned half the time
  - they're so spoiled
  - etc. (fill in with whatever applies to your pupils)
- You may be worried that the administration won't support you.

Those are all understandable reactions. My reply to all of them is:

Get started. After all, what have you got to lose? As you practise these skills you will get better and better at them, and you will find that you have *more* time than before. Teaching will become less stressful and more rewarding.

In the companion volume, "Learning to Listen, Listening to Learn", I discuss how we can further reduce our pupils' resistance to learning new skills and habits. In that book I go into detail to show how we can make it much easier for pupils, particularly those with learning and behaviour problems, to:

- be motivated
- "hear" us
- understand what we expect of them
- remember what to do
- and finally – to do it and to do their best.

You will learn more about how to modify what I call "the language of learning", with the result that your pupils will become more and more ready, willing and able to learn.

I also talk about how we can shift our perspective so that we are able to see school, and in particular our own teaching style, from the "difficult" pupil's point of view. In the process, this pupil becomes calmer, easier and happier and so do we.

About the author

Noël Janis-Norton, founder and director of The New Learning Centre in London, is a learning and behaviour specialist with over 30 years' experience in England and the United States as a teacher, special needs advisor, consultant, lecturer, head teacher and parenting facilitator.

Noël is a mother of two, a foster parent and a grandmother who is passionate about empowering children and adults to fulfil their potential. To achieve this she uses, and teaches parents and professionals to use, her highly effective and thoroughly tested "Calmer, Easier, Happier" parenting and teaching methods.

Her team of skilled, highly experienced teachers and trainers have helped many families whose children are experiencing problems, ranging from mild to severe.

As well as consulting with schools and leading workshops across the UK and in the US, Noël Janis-Norton is still very much a hands-on practitioner. She continues to teach, to work with families and to train professionals. Popular in-service topics for schools are:

- Improving Classroom Behaviour
- Helping the Atypical Learner to Thrive, Not Just Survive
- Preventing and Reducing Bullying
- Involving Parents as Partners in Education
- Raising Standards Through Effective Differentiation
- Harnessing the Learning Strengths of Pupils with Learning Difficulties

For parents, The New Learning Centre offers one-off seminars, ongoing classes and private sessions, both in person and by telephone. Topics include: Effective homework strategies, Maximising co-operation, Motivation and self-reliance, Helping children and teens to express their feelings constructively.

Those who want to explore Noël Janis-Norton's ideas further can contact The New Learning Centre directly:

Address: 211 Sumatra Road, London, NW6 1PF

Telephone: 020 7794 0321

E-mail: admin@tnlc.info

Website: www.tnlc.info